SUMMER
In the Country

The freshest recipes from the country
and easy-breezy ways to enjoy the
simple pleasures of summertime!

Gooseberry Patch
2500 Farmers Dr., #110
Columbus, OH 43235

www.gooseberrypatch.com
1·800·854·6673

Copyright 2008, Gooseberry Patch 978-1-933494-68-5
Sixth Printing, March, 2012

Do you have a tried & true recipe...

tip, craft or memory that you'd like to see featured in a **Gooseberry
Patch** cookbook? Visit our website at **www.gooseberrypatch.com**,
register and follow the easy steps to submit your favorite family recipe.
Or send them to us at:

Gooseberry Patch
Attn: Cookbook Dept.
2500 Farmers Dr., #110
Columbus, OH 43235

Don't forget to include the number of servings your recipe makes,
plus your name, address, phone number and email address.
If we select your recipe, your name will appear right along with
it...and you'll receive a **FREE** copy of the book!

CONTENTS

DEDICATION

To our friends who love sunny afternoons,
swaying in a porch swing, twinkling
fireflies and warm summer breezes.

APPRECIATION

A bit of "Thanks!" to each of you
for sharing your very best
summertime recipes.

Sweet SUMMER Mornings

Pancakes with Blueberry-Cinnamon Syrup

Lori Ritchey
Denver, PA

This recipe is delicious...a combination of good-for-you oats and sweet blueberries.

2 c. milk
1 T. sugar
1-1/2 c. quick-cooking oats, uncooked
1 c. all-purpose flour

2 t. baking powder
1 egg, beaten
2 egg whites, beaten
1/4 c. oil, divided

Mix milk and sugar together in a large bowl; add oats, blending well. In another bowl, blend together flour and baking powder. Add oat mixture, egg, egg whites and 3 tablespoons oil. In a large skillet, heat remaining oil over medium-high heat. Pour batter by 1/4 cupfuls into skillet. Cook pancakes on one side until bubbles appear all over. Flip and continue cooking until golden on other side. Serve warm Blueberry-Cinnamon Syrup. Serves 4 to 6.

Blueberry-Cinnamon Syrup:

2 T. sugar
1 t. cornstarch
1 c. blueberries

1/4 c. water
1 T. lemon juice
3/4 t. cinnamon

Combine sugar and cornstarch in a saucepan over medium heat. Stir in remaining ingredients; bring to a boil.

Light and fizzy...the perfect drink for brunch. Combine one cup sugar, 6 cups chilled pineapple juice and one cup lime juice. Stir in 2 liters sparkling water and serve over crushed ice.

Sweet Summer
MORNINGS

French Toast Croissants

Kathy Grashoff
Fort Wayne, IN

*When summer mornings beckon with so much to do,
this breakfast is quick & easy!*

1/3 c. milk
2 eggs, beaten
1 T. frozen orange juice
   concentrate, thawed

4 croissants, halved lengthwise
Garnish: powdered sugar

Stir milk, eggs and orange juice together in a shallow dish. Dip croissant halves into mixture, turning to coat both sides. Place in a greased skillet over medium heat; cook until golden on both sides. Dust with powdered sugar. Makes 4 servings.

O dandelion, yellow as gold,
What do you do all day?
I just wait here in the tall green grass
Till the children come to play.
-Vintage Children's Reader

Santa Fe Breakfast Bake

Kim Faulkner
Gooseberry Patch

While on vacation, our family found this little, off-the-beaten-path cafe that served an amazing breakfast dish...I ordered it every time! When we returned home, I experimented in the kitchen until I got the recipe just right. Now, whenever I make this, it takes me right back to Santa Fe.

1 c. salsa
1 c. canned black beans, drained and rinsed
10 6-inch corn tortillas, cut into 1-inch strips and divided
1 c. shredded Mexican-blend cheese, divided

1 c. sour cream
1 c. milk
2 eggs, beaten
2 egg whites, beaten
1/2 t. salt
1/4 c. green onions, thinly sliced

Combine salsa and beans; set aside. Place one-third of tortilla strips in a lightly greased 11"x7" baking pan. Top with 1/3 cup cheese and one cup salsa mixture. Repeat layering with one-third of tortilla strips, 1/3 cup cheese and remaining salsa mixture, ending with remaining tortilla strips. Whisk together remaining ingredients. Pour over tortilla strips; sprinkle with remaining cheese. Cover and chill overnight. Remove from refrigerator; let stand at room temperature for 10 minutes. Cover and bake at 350 degrees for 20 minutes. Uncover and bake for an additional 15 minutes, until lightly golden. Serves 6.

Serve breakfast juices in glasses with a bit of sparkle. Run a lemon wedge around the rims of glasses, then dip rims in superfine sugar. Garnish each with a sprig of fresh mint.

Spinach & Potato Frittata

Lynn Williams
Muncie, IN

A tip to remove the moisture from cooked spinach...lay a few paper towels on the counter and place spinach in a single layer on top. Lay another layer or two of paper towels over the spinach, roll and squeeze dry.

6 egg whites, beaten
3 eggs, beaten
1-1/2 c. potato, peeled, diced
   and cooked
2 slices Canadian bacon, diced
6 c. baby spinach, cooked,
   drained and squeezed dry

1/2 t. salt
1/4 t. pepper
1/2 c. onion, chopped
2 T. shredded Cheddar cheese

Whisk together egg whites and eggs in a large bowl. Stir in potato, Canadian bacon, spinach, salt and pepper. Spray a 9" cast-iron skillet with non-stick vegetable spray; place over medium-high heat. Add onion; sauté for 4 minutes until tender. Add potato mixture to pan; cook over medium heat for 5 minutes, or until almost set. Sprinkle with cheese. Bake at 400 degrees for 6 minutes, until set. Let stand for 3 minutes; slice into quarters. Serves 4.

Fresh fruit is perfect pairing with early-morning recipes. Set out plump strawberries, juicy oranges, peach slices and fresh berries to enjoy alongside favorite breakfast dishes. Serve with a bowl of sugar or cream alongside...just to make it extra special.

Grandma Retha's Rhubarb Muffins

Emily Lynch
Iroquois, SD

Five generations of our family have grown up on the same farm for 119 years. We always have lots and lots of rhubarb, and this recipe of Grandma's is an all-time favorite.

1 c. brown sugar, packed
1 egg, beaten
1 c. buttermilk
1/2 c. oil
2 t. vanilla extract
1-1/2 c. rhubarb, diced
Optional: 1/2 c. chopped
    walnuts

2-1/2 c. all-purpose flour
1 t. baking powder
1 t. baking soda
1/2 t. salt
1 t. butter, melted
1/2 c. sugar
1 t. cinnamon

In a large bowl, combine brown sugar, egg, buttermilk, oil and vanilla; mix well. Stir in rhubarb and nuts, if using. In a separate bowl, combine flour, baking powder, baking soda and salt; stir into rhubarb mixture. Spoon into greased muffin tins, filling 2/3 full. Stir together melted butter, sugar and cinnamon; sprinkle over muffins. Bake at 350 degrees for 20 to 25 minutes. Makes 12 to 15 large muffins.

Muffins just seem sweeter served from a create-your-own farmhouse-style muffin stand. Use household cement, found at hardware stores, to secure the bottom of a jadite teacup to the center bottom of a vintage plate. Let cement dry according to the manufacturer's instructions. When completely dry, arrange muffins on the plate, then top with a glass cake stand lid.

Summer's Best Berry Bars

Vickie

*Blueberries are tasty used in this recipe too,
or try mulberries...delectable!*

1 c. quick-cooking oats,
   uncooked
1 c. all-purpose flour
2/3 c. brown sugar, packed

1/4 t. cinnamon
1/8 t. baking soda
1/2 c. butter, melted

Stir together oats, flour, brown sugar, cinnamon and baking soda in
a medium bowl. Stir in butter until well blended; reserve one cup of
mixture for topping. Press remaining oat mixture into an ungreased
9"x9" baking pan. Bake at 350 degrees for 20 to 25 minutes.
Carefully spread berry filling on top of baked crust. Sprinkle with
reserved oat mixture; lightly press into filling. Bake at 350 degrees
for an additional 20 to 25 minutes, until topping is set. Cool in pan
on a wire rack; slice into bars. Makes 1-1/2 dozen.

Berry Filling:

2 c. blackberries, raspberries or
   blueberries
2 T. sugar

2 T. water
1 T. lemon juice
1/2 t. cinnamon

Combine all ingredients in a saucepan over medium heat; bring to a
boil. Reduce heat; simmer, uncovered, for about 8 minutes or until
slightly thickened, stirring frequently. Remove from heat.

Create a light and airy breakfast table setting. Shades of pink,
robin's egg blue, sage green and buttery yellow pair up nicely
with crisp white tablecloths, napkins and dishes.

Last Hurrah of Summer Peach Bread

Jackie Flaherty
Saint Paul, MN

Every late August, I'd take the kids to our family cabin in northern Minnesota for one last week of freedom. On the way home, we'd stop at the small town market and buy Colorado peaches for this recipe. The kids are grown now, but every time I make this bread, I remember all of our joyful trips and how blessed I am. Feel free to use fresh, frozen or canned peaches...all work deliciously.

3 c. all-purpose flour
2 c. sugar
1-1/2 t. salt
1 t. baking soda
4 eggs, beaten
1 c. oil

1 t. vanilla extract
2 t. almond extract
3 to 4 c. peaches, pitted, peeled
    and chopped
Optional: 1 c. chopped nuts

Combine flour, sugar, salt and baking soda in a large bowl; mix well. Add eggs and oil; stir just until moistened. Stir in extracts, peaches and nuts, if using. Spread into 2 greased 9"x5" or four, 7"x4" loaf pans. For regular pans, bake at 350 degrees for 50 to 60 minutes. For small pans, bake for 35 minutes, or until a toothpick comes out clean when inserted near center. Cool for 10 to 15 minutes; remove from pans. Pour glaze over warm loaves. Cool completely. Wrap in wax paper and then aluminum foil. Makes 2 regular or 4 small loaves.

Glaze:

1 T. butter, melted
2 T. milk
1 t. almond extract

1/2 t. vanilla extract
2 c. powdered sugar

Mix all ingredients to make a thin glaze.

Spread slices of quick breads with fruit-flavored
cream cheese...scrumptious!

Just Peachy Coconut Smoothie

Jessica Phillips
Bloomington, IN

My own kitchen creation...the flavors in this smoothie are enjoyed by both adults and children. The natural sweetness from the peaches and honey is divine!

16-oz. pkg. frozen peaches, divided
14-oz. can coconut milk

2 T. honey
2 T. unsweetened flaked coconut
1 t. vanilla extract

Place half the peaches in a blender; reserve remaining peaches for another recipe. Add remaining ingredients to blender; process until smooth and creamy, about 30 seconds. If consistency is too thin, add in a few extra frozen peaches to thicken. Serves 2.

Blueberry-Rhubarb Sauce

Kathy Majeske
Denver, PA

This is a fantastic sauce to serve over pancakes, waffles or even ice cream, and it also freezes well.

6 c. rhubarb, finely chopped
4 c. sugar

21-oz. can blueberry pie filling
3-oz. pkg. raspberry gelatin mix

Combine rhubarb and sugar in a large saucepan over medium heat. Bring to a boil; simmer for 10 minutes. Remove from heat; add pie filling and mix well. Return to heat; bring to a boil. Remove from heat; stir in gelatin mix. Store in jars in refrigerator for up to 4 weeks. Serve warm or cold. Makes 6 cups.

Once known as motel chairs, brightly colored, springy metal chairs are so comfortable and easy to find at flea markets. Pick up a few for the front porch or for a shady spot in the backyard...perfect.

Nellie's Farmgirl Egg Bake

Robin Hill
Rochester, NY

My friend, Nellie, has 18 hens...and when "the girls" are laying lots of eggs, this recipe is one she and I both turn to!

1/2 c. butter, melted
10 eggs, beaten
16-oz. container cottage cheese
16-oz. pkg. shredded
   Monterey Jack cheese

7-oz. can chopped green chiles
1 t. baking powder
1/2 t. salt
1/2 c. all-purpose flour

Drizzle butter evenly into a 13"x9" baking pan. Combine remaining ingredients; mix well and pour into pan. Bake, uncovered, at 350 degrees for 30 minutes. Let stand for 30 minutes before serving. Serves 6 to 8.

An ironstone pitcher filled with old-fashioned lilacs will
bring to mind sweet memories of Grandma's house.
As the season changes, fill pitchers with fragrant
peonies, herb bundles and cheery sunflowers.

Sweet Summer
MORNINGS

Crustless Zucchini Pie

Kathleen Sturm
Corona, CA

This is similar to a quiche, but without the crust. My sisters and their families love this recipe...and we all find it's super when the garden has a bounty of zucchini!

1 onion, finely chopped	1 T. fresh parsley, minced
1/2 c. oil	3 c. zucchini, shredded
1/2 c. grated Parmesan cheese	1 c. biscuit baking mix
4 eggs, beaten	1 c. shredded Cheddar cheese

In a large bowl, combine first 5 ingredients. Stir in remaining ingredients. Pour into two, 9" pie plates that have been sprayed with non-stick vegetable spray. Bake at 350 degrees for 35 to 45 minutes, until golden. Makes 16 servings.

Invite friends over for a farmstyle breakfast served on the porch. Make it summertime-perfect with a yard or two of striped cotton ticking on the table and a milk bottle filled with just-picked posies...it's super simple.

Girls'-Day-Out Granola

Mary Murray
Gooseberry Patch

Each year when Memorial Day comes along, there's a great flea market on the town square not far from where I live. For years, the same group of girlfriends has met there to see what "treasures" we can find to bring home. I always bring along this crunchy-sweet granola mix to share...it keeps our energy up so we don't have to skip a beat of flea-market fun!

4 c. long-cooking oats,
   uncooked
1/2 c. toasted wheat germ
1/2 c. sliced almonds
1/4 c. powdered milk
1/4 c. sunflower seeds
2 T. sesame seed
1-1/2 t. cinnamon
1/4 t. salt

1/2 c. honey
1/4 c. orange juice
1 t. vanilla extract
2 t. oil
1 c. dried mixed fruit, chopped
1 c. golden raisins
1/2 c. sweetened dried
   cranberries

Combine first 8 ingredients in a large bowl; set aside. Combine honey and orange juice in a small saucepan over medium heat; cook for 4 minutes, or until warm. Whisk in vanilla and oil; pour over oat mixture and toss well. Spread mixture into a 15"x10" jelly-roll pan sprayed with non-stick vegetable spray. Bake at 350 degrees for 15 minutes; stir. Bake for an additional 10 minutes, or until crisp. Cool in pan. Place mixture in a large bowl; stir in dried fruits. Makes 8 cups.

When a free morning with girlfriends means barn & tag sales or flea-market shopping, scoop Girls'-Day-Out Granola into easy-to-tote sports bottles...ideal for breakfast on-the-road.

Apple-Berry Breakfast Crisp

Connie Herek
Bay City, MI

Try this with a dollop of vanilla yogurt, yum! I've also used sliced strawberries instead of blueberries and it's just as tasty.

4 apples, cored, peeled and
   thinly sliced
2 c. blueberries
1/4 c. brown sugar, packed
1/4 c. frozen orange juice
   concentrate, thawed

2 T. all-purpose flour
1 t. cinnamon
Optional: vanilla yogurt

Combine all ingredients except yogurt in a large bowl; stir until fruit is evenly coated. Spoon into a lightly greased 8"x8" baking pan. Sprinkle topping evenly over fruit. Bake at 350 degrees for 30 to 35 minutes, until apples are tender. Serve warm with yogurt, if desired. Serves 9.

Topping:

1 c. quick-cooking or long-
   cooking oats, uncooked
1/2 c. brown sugar, packed

1/3 c. butter, melted
2 T. all-purpose flour

Combine all ingredients; mix well.

A sweet topping for
pancakes, waffles, biscuits
or scones....stir a sprinkling
of cinnamon into a cup
of warm honey. Yum!

Friendship Apple Crumpets

Cherry Laird
Maxwell AFB, AL

This is a recipe shared with me by a friend...
it's so good, I make it as often as I can!

3 Gala apples, cored and
   chopped
2 T. vanilla extract
2 T. powdered low-calorie brown
   sugar blend for baking

2 t. cinnamon
1/2 t. allspice
2 16.3-oz. tubes refrigerated
   jumbo whole-wheat
   low-fat biscuits, divided

Combine all ingredients except biscuits in a large bowl. Toss until
apples are well coated; set aside. Reserve 4 biscuits for another recipe.
Flatten remaining biscuits to 1/4-inch thick. Spray a muffin tin with
non-stick vegetable spray or line with paper liners. Lay biscuits flat
over muffin opening; spoon apple mixture onto each biscuit. Use
a spoon to gently push biscuit and mixture into muffin cup. Gather
dough and pinch to seal, covering apples as much as possible.
Sprinkle with additional brown sugar blend and cinnamon, if desired.
Bake at 375 degrees for 10 to 15 minutes. Cool slightly before
serving. Makes one dozen.

Perk up morning place settings in a wink...
fill pint-size jelly jars with gerbera daisies.

Sweet Summer
MORNINGS

Aunt Emmaline's Strawberry Muffins
Dana Cunningham
Lafayette, LA

On the weekend closest to Pioneer Day, our family gathers at my aunt's farmhouse. It's the perfect spot for a get-together...shade trees, tire swings and a porch lined with rocking chairs. The kids, and some grown-ups, like to sleep out under the stars...and when it's time to rise & shine, Aunt Emmaline always has these cream-filled muffins waiting.

1/4 c. cream cheese, softened	1/4 t. salt
2 T. strawberry preserves	2 t. poppy seed
2-1/4 c. all-purpose flour	1-1/4 c. buttermilk
1/3 c. sugar	3 T. oil
2 t. baking powder	2 egg whites, beaten
1/2 t. baking soda	1 egg, beaten

Whisk together cream cheese and preserves in a small bowl; set aside. Combine next 6 ingredients in a medium bowl. Make a well in center of flour mixture and set aside. Whisk remaining ingredients in a large bowl; mix well. Add to flour mixture, stirring just until moistened. Spoon batter into 12 muffin cups sprayed with non-stick vegetable spray, filling 1/3 full. Top each with about one teaspoon cream cheese mixture; divide remaining batter evenly over top. Bake at 375 degrees for 25 minutes, or until muffins spring back when touched lightly in center. Immediately remove muffins from pans; cool on a wire rack. Makes one dozen.

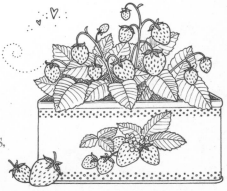

Be on the lookout at flea markets and antique shops for vintage tin bread boxes. Filled with strawberry plants, they're a mini garden patch!

Delicious "Cow Butter"

Shelley Murray-Foley
Waynesville, OH

My children grew up eating this on toast for breakfast.
It's so easy to make and my whole family loves it.

16-oz. pkg. margarine, softened
1 c. buttermilk, at room
  temperature

1/2 c. canola oil
salt to taste

Mix together all ingredients except salt. Whip with an electric mixer on high speed until blended; add salt to taste. Refrigerate until ready to serve. Makes about 3 cups.

Fresh Fruit with Creamy Sauce

Sonya Labbe
Santa Monica, CA

This recipe has always been in my family since I can remember. It's been used with many different fruits depending on what's in season.

1/2 c. vanilla yogurt
1/4 c. unsweetened applesauce
2 t. honey
1 c. apples, cored and sliced
1 c. oranges, peeled and sliced

1 c. strawberries
1 c. blueberries
1 c. raspberries
1 banana, sliced
1/2 c. seedless grapes

Stir together yogurt, applesauce and honey; set aside. Toss together fruit in a large bowl; divide among 6 dessert dishes. Spoon sauce over top. Makes 6 servings.

Create a shady spot on the porch with full-length shutters...simply
hinge together two or three, stand them together to make
a screen, then enjoy breakfast in the shade.

Spoon Bread

Tina Goodpasture
Meadowview, VA

*This is wonderful...it brings back memories of my childhood when
my Granny Hudson made "Morning Bread" for our breakfast.
I use fresh cornmeal that is ground at a local grist mill.*

1 c. cornmeal
3 c. milk, divided
3 eggs, beaten

2 t. baking powder
1 T. butter, melted
2 t. salt

Combine cornmeal and 2 cups milk in a saucepan over medium heat;
bring to a boil, stirring constantly. Add remaining milk, eggs, baking
powder, butter and salt. Pour into a greased one-quart casserole dish.
Bake at 400 degrees for about 35 minutes, or until a knife inserted in
the center comes out clean. Serve warm. Serves 4 to 6.

Think flea-market fresh when decorating the kitchen for
summer. An enamelware colander filled with soil can hold a
collection of herbs or pretty pansies, while a vintage child-size
watering can is the perfect size for just-picked garden blooms.

Ericka's Cheese Danish

Ericka McIntosh
Blackshear, GA

When creamy cheese Danish is what you're craving,
this quick-fix favorite is sure to please!

2 8-oz. tubes refrigerated
   crescent rolls
2 8-oz. pkgs. cream cheese,
   softened

3/4 c. plus 1 T. sugar, divided
1 egg, separated
1 t. vanilla extract

Layer one tube crescent rolls in a greased 13"x9" inch baking pan; press seams together. Blend together cream cheese, 3/4 cup sugar, egg yolk and vanilla; spread over dough. Top with remaining tube of crescent rolls. Brush with egg white; sprinkle with remaining sugar. Bake at 350 degrees for 30 minutes. Slice into squares. Serves 6 to 8.

Strawberries make a sweet summertime side for any meal. To keep them their freshest, don't wash them until ready to use. Place in a bowl and store in the coldest part of the refrigerator, loosely covered with plastic wrap, for up to 3 days.

Lemon Fluff

Alissa Post
Scottsdale, AZ

This dip is delicious served with watermelon, grapes, cantaloupe, bananas, apples...just about any type of fruit. My family can't get enough of it during the summer months!

2.9-oz. pkg. cook & serve lemon pudding mix
3/4 c. sugar, divided
2 egg yolks

2-1/4 c. water, divided
1 pt. whipping cream
1 t. lemon extract
assorted fresh fruit, sliced

Whisk together pudding mix, 1/2 cup sugar, egg yolks and 1/4 cup water in a medium saucepan; mix well. Add remaining water. Whisking constantly, cook over medium heat until mixture comes to a full boil. Remove from heat; cool to room temperature, stirring occasionally to keep smooth. In a separate bowl, with an electric mixer on high speed, beat cream with remaining sugar and lemon extract until peaks form. Fold in pudding mixture; refrigerate for 2 to 3 hours, or overnight. Serve with assorted fresh fruit. Makes 20 to 25 servings.

Amy's Orange Shake-Up

Amy Maletto
Saint Marys, PA

When my children were little and were sick, I would always make this delicious drink for them to "make them better." We also enjoy it on family movie nights with popcorn. It's such a hit, my daughter presented a school project on our family and "the best drink ever!"

6-oz. can frozen orange juice concentrate, partially thawed
1 c. milk
1 c. water

1/2 c. sugar
1 t. vanilla extract
10 to 12 ice cubes

Combine all ingredients except ice cubes into a blender. Add ice cubes 2 at a time; process until smooth. Pour into tall glasses. Makes 4 servings.

Sweet Pea's Breakfast Blitz

Kimberly Wines
Front Royal, VA

When I was a young girl I would spend many weekend nights with my Grandma Susie, nicknamed "Sweet Pea." She would always serve a special breakfast that I have served to my own children for many years. Her recipe brings back many wonderful family memories of me and my "Sweet Pea." It will surely awaken your little ones' eyes as well as their taste buds.

4 eggs
1 to 2 T. cider vinegar
1 t. butter, softened

salt and pepper to taste
2 English muffins, split and
   toasted

Cover eggs with water in a small saucepan over high heat. Bring to a boil; cook for 15 minutes. While eggs are still warm, peel and chop; place in a bowl. Stir in vinegar, butter, salt and pepper. Spoon onto toast or English muffins. Makes 2 servings.

Serve up cool and refreshing fruit-flavored waters...it's so easy. Slice apples or strawberries into thin slivers and slip into bottled water. Let them chill so the fruit gently flavors the water, and drink within one day. Try adding mint sprigs or ripe peach slices too!

Country-Style Breakfast Pizza

Jackie Balla
Walbridge, OH

A sure-fire breakfast hit...you'll get requests for this recipe!

13.8-oz. tube refrigerated pizza dough
Optional: garlic salt
24-oz. pkg. refrigerated mashed potatoes
10 eggs, beaten

Optional: chopped vegetables, cooked ham or sausage
8-oz. pkg. shredded Colby Jack cheese
4-oz. pkg. crumbled bacon pieces

Spread pizza dough in a pizza pan; sprinkle with garlic salt, if desired, and set aside. Place mashed potatoes in a microwave-safe bowl; microwave on high setting for about 5 minutes, or until heated through. Spread potatoes over dough. Scramble eggs as desired, adding vegetables, sausage or ham, if desired. Spread scrambled eggs evenly over potatoes. Sprinkle with cheese; top with bacon. Bake at 350 degrees for 30 minutes, or until cheese is melted and bubbly. Makes 8 servings.

Surprise sleepyheads at breakfast...serve each a made-to-order omelet in a mini cast-iron skillet. A cheery red bandanna tied around the handle makes a nice, big napkin.

Herbed Salmon Omelets

Carrie O'Shea
Marina Del Rey, CA

My husband's brother lives in Alaska, and last summer our family reunion was held there. The men went fishing all day, and the ladies crafted, shopped and tried to find new ways to prepare the bounty of fish being brought home! This recipe was one we enjoyed many times... it's delicious and couldn't be easier to make.

1/4 c. sour cream
2 T. fresh dill, chopped
2 T. fresh chives, chopped
2 T. butter, divided

1/4 lb. smoked salmon, chopped
  and divided
6 eggs, beaten and divided

Mix together sour cream and herbs in a small bowl; set aside. Heat one tablespoon butter in a skillet over low heat. Add half the salmon; cook and stir for one minute. Add half the eggs to skillet and cook, lifting edges to allow uncooked egg to flow underneath. When almost set, spoon half the sour cream mixture over half the omelet. Fold other half over and slide onto plate. Keep warm while making second omelet with remaining ingredients. Serves 2.

Cheese toast is delicious alongside savory breakfast dishes...
and a snap to make on a countertop grill. Spread softened
butter over slices of Italian or sourdough bread, grill
until golden, then sprinkle with Parmesan cheese.

Friendship
GARDEN
Brunch

for you!

Tomatoes

Farmhouse Quiche

Jo Ann

*Fresh tasting and packed with flavor, this is one recipe I make
for our whole family all summer long.*

9-inch pie crust
2 T. olive oil
1/2 red pepper, diced
1/2 green pepper, diced
2 cloves garlic, minced
1/4 c. zucchini, diced
2 T. fresh basil, chopped
4 eggs, beaten

1 c. half-and-half
1 t. salt
1/2 t. pepper
8-oz. pkg. shredded Pepper Jack
   cheese
1/3 c. shredded Parmesan
   cheese
3 plum tomatoes, sliced

Pierce bottom and sides of pie crust with a fork. Bake at 425 degrees
for 10 minutes; set aside. Heat oil in a large skillet over medium heat;
sauté peppers, garlic, zucchini and basil until tender. Whisk together
eggs, half-and-half, salt and pepper in a large bowl. Stir in vegetables
and cheeses. Pour into pie crust and top with sliced tomatoes. Bake
at 375 degrees for 45 minutes. Let stand 5 minutes before slicing.
Makes 6 servings.

Invite friends to come for a plant swap...what fun! Deliver
invitations (tucked inside gardening gloves) and be sure to
ask that they bring along plants from their own gardens
to share...what a good excuse to dig in the dirt!

Orange-Walnut Brunch Cake

Jackie Smulski
Lyons, IL

*Don't save this yummy cake just for special occasions...
enjoy it anytime!*

17.3-oz. tube refrigerated jumbo
   biscuits
1/4 c. walnuts, finely chopped
1/3 c. sugar
1 T. orange zest

2 T. butter, melted
1/2 c. powdered sugar
3 T. cream cheese, softened
2 T. orange juice

Grease a 9" round cake pan. Separate biscuit dough into 8 biscuits.
Place one biscuit in center of pan. Cut remaining biscuits in half,
forming 14 half-circles. Arrange pieces around center biscuit, with
cut sides facing same direction. Combine walnuts, sugar and orange
zest in a small bowl; mix well. Brush butter over tops of biscuits and
sprinkle with walnut mixture. Bake at 375 degrees for 20 minutes,
or until golden. In a separate bowl, combine powdered sugar, cream
cheese and enough orange juice for desired drizzling consistency.
Blend until smooth; drizzle over warm cake. Cool for 10 minutes.
Serve warm. Serves 6 to 8.

Edible flowers are such pretty cake toppers...choose pesticide-free
blooms such as pansies, violets, chamomile, lavender, nasturtiums and
hollyhocks. Before using, rinse and gently shake each flower under
running water, then set aside to drain and dry on paper towels.

Dressed-Up Egg Salad

Robin Hill
Rochester, NY

Filled with smoked salmon and capers...this is the recipe I prepare when the girls and I are getting together for brunch.

6 eggs, hard-boiled, peeled and chopped
2 ozs. smoked salmon, finely chopped
1 t. dill weed
1 t. capers
1/4 c. mayonnaise
1 t. salt
1 t. pepper
1 stalk celery, finely chopped
1 green onion, chopped
14 slices country-style white bread, lightly toasted

Combine all ingredients except bread in a large bowl; mix until well combined. Spread 1/4 cup egg mixture over half of bread slices; top with remaining bread slices. Trim crusts, if desired. Makes 7 servings.

Toss pillows for outdoor furniture are easy to make using two cotton tea towels and hem tape. Press iron-on hem tape on the wrong side of one towel, then remove the paper backing. Lay the second tea towel on top, wrong sides together, and press, leaving an opening for a pillow. Slip the pillow inside, then press the openings together.

Carolina Spinach Salad

Laura Fuller
Fort Wayne, IN

This salad recipe is one our family discovered on a trip to Charleston, South Carolina a few summers ago. You'll need to prepare the dressing several days ahead, then refrigerate. When the salad is ready to serve, shake the dressing very well for 15 to 30 seconds before using.

8 c. baby spinach
2 c. seedless green grapes
1 lb. cooked medium shrimp
1 c. celery, thinly sliced
1 c. jicama, peeled and thinly
    sliced

1/2 cucumber, thinly sliced
1/4 c. green onions, sliced
2 t. toasted sesame seed

Toss together all ingredients except sesame seed in a large bowl. Add dressing to taste. Serve on 8 individual plates. Sprinkle each serving with sesame seed. Serves 8.

Homemade Sesame Vinaigrette Dressing:

1/4 c. rice vinegar
2 T. olive oil
1 T. toasted sesame oil
1 T. sugar
1 t. garlic, minced

1 t. fresh ginger, peeled and
    grated
1/2 t. salt
1/2 t. pepper

Combine all ingredients in a blender. Cover and blend well.

A sweet summertime glow...fill plain glass votive candleholders with coarse salt, then tuck in a votive. The salt crystals will sparkle in the flickering light.

Mango Chutney Chicken Bites

Lisanne Miller
Canton, MS

This is a fantastic summertime appetizer...a tasty, lighter version of chicken salads that contain mayonnaise. So quick & easy and once your family & friends get a taste, they'll want more!

12-1/2 oz. can chicken, drained
2 to 3 T. mango chutney
1/8 t. ground ginger
1/8 t. pepper

2 T. green onions chopped
crackers or thinly sliced French
   bread
Garnish: chopped green onions

Mix all ingredients together except garnish and crackers; cover and refrigerate overnight. Serve on crackers or thinly sliced French bread; sprinkle with green onion. Makes 3 to 4 dozen.

Pretty vintage aprons can be found for a song at flea markets, why not tie one on the back of each chair surrounding the brunch table? A sweet way to say "Thanks for coming!"

Crunchy Strawberry Salad

Lori Rosenberg
Cleveland, OH

This terrific salad is a combination of crunchy, sweet and tangy... everyone will love it!

3-oz. pkg. ramen noodles
2 T. butter
1 c. chopped walnuts
1/4 c. oil
2 T. powdered calorie-free
   sweetener

2 T. red wine vinegar
1/2 t. soy sauce
8 c. romaine lettuce, torn
1/2 c. green onions, chopped
2 c. strawberries, hulled and
   sliced

Discard seasoning packet from ramen noodles or save for another use. Break noodles into small pieces. Heat butter in a large skillet over medium heat. Add noodles and walnuts. Sauté until golden, about 8 to 10 minutes; cool. For dressing, combine oil, sweetener, vinegar and soy sauce in an airtight container; shake well. Just before serving, combine lettuce, onions, strawberries and noodle mixture in a large bowl. Drizzle with dressing and toss gently. Makes 12 servings.

Welcome friends to brunch by setting a pretty table. Use favorite collections, vintage tablecloths and napkins, mismatched silver and glassware in colorful shades of summer.

Lime & Cilantro Cornish Game Hens

Jaime Hughes
Yucca Valley, CA

My mom used to make this every year when I came home from summer camp as my Welcome Home dinner. The aroma was so nice to come home to! This recipe will always remind me of those summer days and my sweet mom who was happily waiting for me at home with my favorite meal.

4 Cornish game hens, or
    4 boneless, skinless
    chicken breasts
12 limes

1 bunch fresh cilantro, chopped
salt and pepper to taste
cooked rice

Place each hen into a one-gallon plastic zipping bag. If using chicken breasts, place all pieces into a one-gallon plastic zipping bag. Squeeze juice of 3 limes into each bag; add one-quarter of cilantro to each bag. Add salt and pepper. Refrigerate overnight. Remove hens or chicken breasts from bags, discard marinade. Bake at 350 degrees for one hour, or until juices run clear. If baking chicken breasts, bake for 20 to 25 minutes. Serve over white rice. Serves 4.

Share a potted rosemary herb plant with friends. As a symbol of remembrance, it's a sweet way of letting them know you care.

Friendship
GARDEN BRUNCH

Cranberry-Dijon Chicken

Jackie Smulski
Lyons, IL

*Tangy with a hint of sweetness...I like to keep supper easy by
just adding a simple side of rice and a green salad.*

1/2 c. whole-berry cranberry
   sauce
2 T. Dijon mustard
1 T. sugar

pepper to taste
4 boneless, skinless chicken
   breasts

Combine all ingredients except chicken in a large bowl; mix well.
Add chicken; turn to coat evenly. Spray a grill pan with non-stick
vegetable spray. Remove chicken from cranberry mixture; discard
mixture. Grill over medium heat for 3 to 4 minutes per side, until
juices run clear. Serves 4.

When it's time to divide and share perennials, make sure to
label each plant with its name, how tall it will grow, does
it like sun or shade and any other suggestions for
making a new friendship garden grow!

Sweet Pineapple with Basil

Kay Barg
Sandy, UT

A fresh-tasting, summery recipe...fresh basil adds just the right flavor.

1 pineapple, peeled, cored and
    cut into bite-size pieces
2 T. sugar

2 t. lemon juice, or to taste
1/4 c. fresh basil, chopped
Garnish: additional fresh basil

In a large bowl, gently toss pineapple with sugar, lemon juice and
chopped basil. Serve garnished with additional basil. Makes
8 servings.

Visit a barn sale to find oodles of ideas for bringing whimsy to the
garden! Plant herbs or flowers in a pair of cast-off garden boots,
washstands, wheelbarrows or leaky watering cans.

Friendship
GARDEN BRUNCH

Pecan-Kiwi Salad

Diane Hixon
Niceville, FL

A crunchy, fruity salad you'll find yourself making all summer long.

5 c. Boston lettuce, torn
3 kiwis, peeled and sliced
1/4 c. chopped pecans, toasted
2 T. vanilla yogurt

2 T. lemon juice
1 T. oil
1 T. honey

Combine lettuce, kiwis and pecans in a large bowl; set aside. Mix together remaining ingredients in a small bowl, stirring until smooth. Pour over salad; toss gently. Makes 4 to 6 servings.

Set a farm table with lightweight fiber pots, pails of soil, plant markers and watering cans...a gardening workstation that makes it so easy to divide and pot new plants for swapping

Grandma Hilda's Sweet Biscuits

Reggie Jarvi
Hancock, MI

Every summer at the end of July, it was our family's tradition to travel to "Little Grandma's" farm to help with the hay-making. On the farm, we had the freedom to chase fireflies or chickens, milk the cows and ride the "old joker"...the truck which was used to pull the hay wagon to the barn. We always looked forward to having these biscuits with every meal.

6 c. all-purpose flour
1 c. sugar
1 t. salt
3 T. plus 1 t. baking powder

1 c. shortening
3 eggs, beaten
1 c. milk

Mix together first 5 ingredients in a large bowl; mix well. In a separate bowl, beat eggs and milk together. Add to flour mixture and blend well. Roll out on a floured surface; cut with 3-inch round cookie cutter. Bake at 375 degrees for 15 to 20 minutes, until golden. Makes 4 dozen.

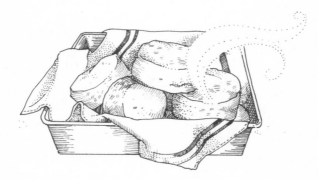

Try this delicious berry & honey spread on warm biscuits. Combine one pint stemmed strawberries, one tablespoon lemon juice and 1/2 cup honey in a blender until smooth. Pour into a saucepan and simmer over low heat 20 minutes; stirring occasionally. Makes 1-1/2 cups.

Garden Path Herbal Bread

Brenda Smith
Gooseberry Patch

When we moved out to the country, I began tucking a few herb plants here & there in my flower gardens. I enjoyed cooking with them so much, I planted herbs all along the edge of a path that leads from my back door to the barn!

1 c. all-purpose flour	2 T. Dijon mustard
2 t. baking powder	1/2 c. grated Parmesan cheese
1/2 t. salt	1/4 c. fresh oregano, minced
3 eggs, beaten	1/4 c. fresh chives, minced
1 c. plain yogurt	1/4 c. fresh thyme, minced

Stir together flour, baking powder, salt, eggs, yogurt and mustard in a large bowl; blend well. Add cheese and herbs; mix well. Pour batter into an 8"x4" loaf pan that has been sprayed with non-stick vegetable spray. Bake at 400 degrees for 45 minutes. Turn out bread on a wire rack to cool. Makes one loaf.

Tuck flowers into clever containers. Watering cans, vintage metal lunchboxes, enamelware pots & pans... even a tin cup makes the sweetest planter.

Bubbly Zucchini-Mozzarella Casserole

Donna Fannin
Fairfield, OH

Everyone seems to love this casserole...the combination
of flavors just can't be beat.

2 zucchini, sliced
1 yellow squash, sliced
3 4-oz. cans sliced mushrooms,
   drained
2 14-1/2 oz. cans diced Italian
   tomatoes with olive oil

Italian seasoning to taste
8-oz. pkg. sliced pepperoni
8-oz. pkg. shredded mozzarella
   cheese

Layer zucchini and squash in a lightly greased 13"x9" baking pan.
Top with mushrooms and tomatoes; sprinkle with Italian seasoning.
Top with pepperoni. Bake, covered, at 350 degrees for about one hour,
until pepperoni is golden and vegetables are tender. Sprinkle with
cheese; bake for an additional 10 minutes, or until cheese is melted.
Serves 8.

Herbal sun tea is refreshing and so easy to make. Place 4 to
6 teabags in a 2-quart glass container filled with water and
secure the lid. Place outside in the sunlight for 3 to 5 hours.
Pour servings into ice-filled glasses and add sugar to taste...ahhh.

Friendship
GARDEN BRUNCH

Rosemary's Layered Tomato-Pesto Bake

Missie Brown
Gooseberry Patch

When my friend, Rosemary, found bunches of basil too good to pass up at the farmers' market, she made homemade pesto for this recipe... it's really easier to make than you might think!

1 loaf sourdough bread, sliced
   1/2-inch thick
8-oz. pkg. cream cheese, cubed
8-oz. pkg. shredded mozzarella
   cheese
3/4 c. basil pesto sauce
5-oz. pkg. prosciutto or deli
   ham, thinly sliced

1 lb. tomatoes, thinly sliced
5 eggs, beaten
1-1/2 c. half-and-half
1/2 t. salt
pepper to taste

Arrange half the bread slices in a 2-quart casserole dish that has been sprayed with non-stick vegetable spray. Layer with half each of cream cheese, mozzarella, pesto, prosciutto or ham and tomatoes. Make one more layer with remaining ingredients. Whisk together eggs, half-and-half, salt and pepper. Pour over layers; cover and chill for at least 2 hours to overnight. Remove from refrigerator 20 to 30 minutes before baking. Bake, uncovered, at 350 degrees for one hour, until puffed, golden and lightly set in center. Let stand for 10 minutes. Run a knife along edges to loosen. Place a serving plate over top and carefully invert. Repeat inverting so that strata is right-side up. Makes 6 servings.

Freeze this summer's fresh basil to enjoy it all year long. Combine 1/4 cup olive oil with 2 cups packed basil leaves in a food processor. Pulse until finely chopped, spoon into an ice cube tray and freeze. Once the cubes are frozen, place in a plastic freezer bag and return to the freezer...great for flavoring soups, sauces and salad dressings.

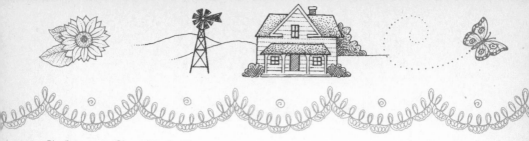

Salmon-Stuffed Tomatoes

Sylvia Mathews
Vancouver, WA

Traditional stuffed tomatoes "dressed-up" with salmon and capers.

1 tomato, halved
1/2 lb. salmon, chopped
1/3 c. bread crumbs
1/2 c. fresh Italian parsley,
   chopped

1 t. olive oil
1 clove garlic, chopped
1 to 2 t. capers, chopped

Scoop out and discard tomato pulp; set aside. Combine remaining ingredients; evenly spoon into tomato halves. Place on a lightly greased baking sheet. Bake at 350 degrees for 30 minutes. Serves 2.

What a time-saver...the serrated edges of a grapefruit spoon
are so handy when it's time to hollow out tomatoes!

42

Friendship
GARDEN BRUNCH

Heather's BLT Bites

Heather Werner
Paxton, IL

I discovered this recipe when my husband was in the military. He loved it and I always made it for him when he came home from long tours. Now, he travels a lot for work, but he still comes home to these little bites after he's been away. A true family favorite.

1 lb. bacon, crisply cooked and
    crumbled
1 c. mayonnaise-type salad
    dressing

1-1/2 c. green onions, chopped
1/2 c. grated Parmesan cheese
10 to 12 roma tomatoes

Stir together bacon, salad dressing, onions and Parmesan until well blended; set aside. Cut a small slice from the top of each tomato; scoop out and discard pulp of tomatoes. Fill each tomato with bacon mixture; refrigerate for one hour. Makes 10 to 12.

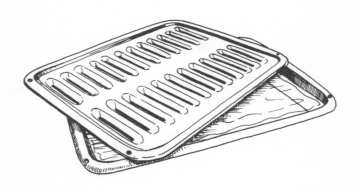

To prepare crispy bacon easily, try baking it in the oven. Place
bacon slices on a broiler pan, place the pan in the oven and turn
the temperature to 400 degrees. Bake for 12 to 15 minutes,
turn bacon over and bake for another 8 to 10 minutes.

43

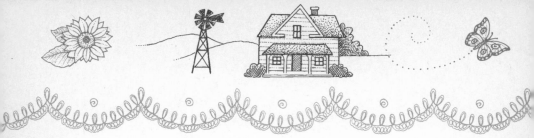

Lemony Orzo Salad

Doreen Freiman
Lake Hiawatha, NJ

I make this for every outdoor summer party...it brings back so many great memories of all the good times spent with friends & family.

16-oz. pkg. orzo pasta,
    uncooked
3 to 4 c. baby spinach, torn into
    bite-size pieces
1/4 c. olive oil
1/2 c. lemon juice
2 T. garlic powder
2 T. onion powder

2 t. fresh parsley, chopped, or
    1 t. dried parsley
1 t. salt
1 t. pepper
2-1/4 oz. can sliced black olives,
    drained
1 c. grape tomatoes

Cook pasta just until tender; drain. Place spinach in a large bowl; add hot pasta and let stand for 2 to 3 minutes to wilt spinach. Combine remaining ingredients except olives and tomatoes. Mix well; add to pasta. Stir in olives and tomatoes. Serve either warm or chilled. Serves 8 to 10.

Serve salads in an unexpected, garden-fresh salad bowl...
a hollowed-out head of cabbage, or spoon individual
servings into pitted avocado halves.

Summery Chicken & Rice Salad

Kay Johnson
Muskegon, MI

This wonderful summertime lunch recipe was shared with me by my mother-in-law years ago. We like to serve it with fresh fruit and homemade banana bread or hard rolls. I like to start preparing it the night before, then just stir in the last 4 ingredients before serving time. You really have to try it!

2 c. cooked chicken breast,
   cubed
1-1/2 c. cooked rice
1/2 c. pineapple chunks
2 T. oil
1 t. salt

1 c. celery, chopped
1/4 c. green pepper, chopped
3/4 c. chopped pecans
1/2 c. to 3/4 c. mayonnaise
Garnish: lettuce leaves

Combine chicken, rice, pineapple, oil and salt in a large bowl; chill for at least 2 hours. Fold in celery, green pepper and pecans; add mayonnaise to taste. Spoon into a lettuce-lined serving bowl. Makes 10 to 12 servings.

Tag and barn sales can turn up the prettiest vintage
cotton picnic cloths...hang one across any window
for an instant fresh farmhouse look!

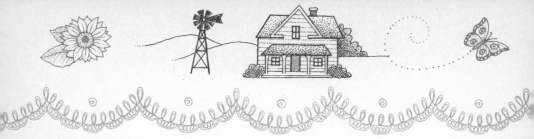

My Favorite Greek Salad

Denise Neal
Castle Rock, CO

I love Greek food and this is one of my favorite recipes...it brings back memories of my vacation to the Greek Islands. I love to use my garden's red and yellow heirloom variety of tomatoes in the summer. For some extra crunch, toss in diced celery.

1 cucumber, peeled and diced
2 tomatoes, diced
1/2 red onion, thinly sliced
1/2 c. pitted Kalamata olives
1/2 c. crumbled feta cheese

3 T. olive oil
2 T. lemon juice
1 t. dried oregano
1/8 t. salt
1/8 t. sugar

Combine vegetables and cheese in a large bowl. Whisk together remaining ingredients; toss gently with salad. Refrigerate until ready to serve. Makes 4 servings.

Turn clay flower pots upside-down and line up along the edge of a garden path or flower bed...clever!

Heavenly Herb Dip with Pita Chips

Michelle Rooney
Gooseberry Patch

So simple to whip up, and you may as well make a
double batch at the start...this won't last long.

1 cucumber, coarsely chopped
1 red onion, chopped
2 4-oz. containers crumbled
   feta cheese
1 T. olive oil

2-1/2 T. lemon juice
3 T. fresh dill, chopped
3 T. fresh mint, chopped
Garnishes: fresh mint leaves,
   lemon wedges

Combine cucumber, onion and cheese in a medium bowl. Sprinkle
with oil, juice and herbs; toss to mix. Garnish as desired; serve with
pita chips. Makes 6 servings.

Pita Chips:

3 pita rounds
3 T. olive oil

1/4 t. salt
1/4 t. pepper

Split pita rounds; cut each round into 8 wedges. Brush oil over both
sides of wedges; sprinkle with salt and pepper. Arrange wedges in a
single layer on a lightly greased baking sheet. Bake at 375 degrees for
6 minutes on each side, until crisp.

Serve up a side salad in no time...
combine a bag of spring mix
lettuce with fresh baby spinach.
Toss with mandarin oranges,
almonds and red onion rings, then
drizzle with a favorite dressing.

Stuffed Strawberries

Lisa Ann Panzino DiNunzio
Vineland, NJ

A perfect summertime starter for any get-together. Choose the plumpest, largest berries you can find.

20 large strawberries, hulled and divided
8-oz. pkg. cream cheese, softened

1 T. powdered sugar

Hull and dice 2 strawberries; set aside. Cut a thin slice from stem end of remaining strawberries, forming a base so berries can stand upright. Starting at the opposite end of strawberries, slice into 4 wedges being careful not to slice all the way through; set aside. Beat together cream cheese and sugar until well blended; fold in diced strawberries. Spoon 1-1/2 tablespoonfuls of cream cheese mixture into center of each strawberry. Arrange on a serving platter; refrigerate until ready to serve. Makes 6 to 8 servings.

Ice cream shortcakes for dessert...in just minutes! Halve 2 biscuits, then toss 2 sliced nectarines with 1/2 cup peach preserves. Top each biscuit with half the mixture and a dollop of peach ice cream...so delicious!

Friendship
GARDEN BRUNCH

Apple Berry Salsa & Cinnamon Chips

Gigi Berrett
Orem, UT

A friend gave me this recipe at least 10 years ago.
Always a hit, it's easy to make and so delicious.

2 apples, cored, peeled and
   chopped
1 c. strawberries, hulled and
   coarsely chopped
1 to 2 kiwis, peeled and coarsely
   chopped

zest and juice of 1 orange,
   divided
2 T. brown sugar, packed
2 T. apple jelly

Combine apples, strawberries, kiwis and zest in a large bowl. Mix juice, sugar and jelly in a small bowl; add to fruit. Serve immediately, or chill until ready to serve. Serve with cinnamon chips. Makes 8 servings.

Cinnamon Chips:

6 8-inch flour tortillas
2 T. sugar

1 t. cinnamon

Spray both sides of each tortilla with non-stick vegetable spray. Slice each tortilla into wedges. Combine sugar and cinnamon in a large plastic zipping bag. Place tortilla wedges in bag; seal and shake to coat. Arrange wedges on a lightly greased baking sheet. Bake at 375 degrees for 8 to 10 minutes, until crisp and golden.

Add a bit of whimsy to
welcome family & friends...
make a daisy chain garland
to hang on the garden gate!

Strawberry Lemonade

Shaelei Davenport
Portland, TX

This is great for cooling off on those hot summer days here in Texas.

1 qt. strawberries, hulled
3 c. cold water
3/4 c. sugar

3/4 c. lemon juice
2 c. club soda, chilled

Place strawberries, water, and sugar in a blender; process until smooth. Pour into a pitcher. Stir in lemon juice and soda; serve immediately. Makes 2 quarts.

Creamy Coffee Granita

Penny Sherman
Cumming, GA

Start this about 3 hours before you'd like to serve it.

6 c. hot, strong brewed coffee
1/2 c. sugar

Garnish: whipped cream

Pour coffee and sugar into a 13"x9" baking pan, stirring to dissolve sugar. Cover with plastic wrap; place in freezer. Freeze for 3 hours, scraping occasionally, until frozen. Serve topped with whipped cream. Serves 8 to 10.

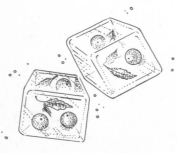

Garnish summer beverages with fruit-flavored ice cubes. Cut favorite fruits like watermelon, cantaloupe, kiwi or honeydew melon into cubes, purée in a food processor and freeze in ice cube trays.

An Old-Fashioned PICNIC

Beverly's Fried Chicken

Beverly Ray
Brandon, FL

I used to make this recipe when we took our family vacations in the summertime. We'd stop off at a pretty rest stop, throw out a blanket and have an on-the-road picnic. My family always enjoyed strawberry preserves and butter sandwiches with fried chicken.

1 c. canola oil	1 t. pepper
2 c. all-purpose flour	2 to 3 lbs. chicken
1 t. salt	

Combine flour, salt and pepper in a brown paper grocery bag. Add 2 to 3 pieces chicken at a time to bag; shake to coat. Repeat until all of chicken is coated. Heat oil in a large electric or cast-iron skillet over medium-high heat. Fry chicken over medium-high heat until golden on both sides, turning frequently, for 45 to 50 minutes, until juices run clear. Makes 4 to 6 servings.

For the crispiest fried chicken, start in the morning. Combine
2 tablespoons salt and one cup of warm water in a large bowl;
stir to dissolve the salt. Add chicken to the bowl, cover with very
cold water and add a tray of ice cubes. Chill in the refrigerator
until dinner time, then drain, pat dry and fry.

An Old-Fashioned
PICNIC

Country-Style Baked Potato Salad

Deanna Lyons
Gooseberry Patch

A truly tasty salad...a spin on a loaded baked potato.
Use any or all of your favorite toppings!

4 lbs. baking potatoes, peeled,
 cubed and cooked
1 lb. bacon, sliced into 1/2-inch
 pieces and crisply cooked
8-oz. pkg. shredded Cheddar
 cheese

1/2 c. butter, softened
1/2 c. green onions, chopped
1-1/2 c. sour cream
1 t. salt
1 t. pepper

Combine all ingredients in a large bowl, tossing gently. Chill for
2 hours before serving. Makes 10 to 12 servings.

Whip up a fresh salad dressing for any tossed salad...in a jiffy!
Whisk together 1/2 cup raspberry spreadable fruit,
1/3 cup raspberry vinegar, 1 tablespoon honey,
1 tablespoon poppy seed and 1 cup canola oil.

Jen's Pulled Pork

Jennifer Inacio
Hummelstown, PA

A recipe I created, this is now one of my most requested dishes for picnics! I use diet cola, as it's less sweet in flavor. There's no right or wrong to how much sauce to use...simply stir in as much as you'd like. A friend of mine adds sliced jalapeños, minced garlic or sautéed onions and green peppers.

3 to 4-lb. boneless pork loin
   roast, halved
2-ltr. bottle diet cola

2 28-oz. bottles honey barbecue
   sauce
8 to 10 hamburger buns, split

Place roast into a slow cooker fat-side up; add cola. Cover and cook on low setting for 12 to 14 hours. Remove from slow cooker; remove and discard any fat. Discard cooking liquids; wipe slow cooker with a paper towel. Shred pork and return to slow cooker; add barbecue sauce to taste. Cover and cook on low setting for an additional hour, until heated through. Add more sauce, if desired. Serve on buns. Serves 8 to 10.

Keep picnics festive and comfy...bring along colorful, soft quilts and blankets for lunch in the shade. Once lunch is over, those soft and cozy quilts also create a perfect spot for napping!

Super Hero Sandwich

Machelle Anderson
Central City, NE

This sandwich can be prepared ahead of time and stored in the fridge until you are ready to bake. It's always a crowd pleaser.

1 loaf French bread
2 T. butter, softened and divided
1/2 lb. deli ham, sliced
6 ozs. provolone cheese, sliced
  and divided

4 T. Italian salad dressing,
  divided
1/4 lb. deli turkey, sliced
1/4 lb. deli salami, sliced
1 T. butter, melted

Split bread horizontally into 3 equal slices. Place bottom layer of bread on a sheet of aluminum foil large enough to cover entire sandwich. Spread bottom layer with one tablespoon butter. Top with ham and half the cheese; drizzle with 2 tablespoons salad dressing. Place second layer of bread on top. Spread with remaining butter; top with turkey, salami, remaining cheese and remaining salad dressing. Place remaining layer of bread on top; brush with melted butter. Fold aluminum foil to completely wrap sandwich. Place on a baking sheet. Bake at 400 degrees for 15 minutes. Slice as desired. Makes 6 servings.

To make picnics kid-friendly, tuck lunches into summertime sand pails. Fill each pail with a wrapped peanut butter & jelly sandwich, kid-size bag of potato chips and a cookie. After lunch, the pail is perfect for holding all kinds of goodies.

Grandma Alice's Tomato Salad

Diana Strawbridge
Ashtabula, OH

Alice was my grandmother and a wonderful cook. Grandma always made this delicious salad in the summer from the fresh tomatoes she picked from her garden. We have enjoyed it so many times over the years, as it continues to remind me of her.

7 tomatoes, thinly sliced	1/2 c. white vinegar
1 yellow onion, thinly sliced	1/2 c. oil
1/2 c. sugar	salt and pepper to taste

Combine tomatoes and onion in a large bowl. In a separate bowl, combine remaining ingredients. Pour over tomatoes and onion; toss gently. Let stand at room temperature for up to one hour before serving. Serves 6.

If time's short, pick up a bag of tossed salad greens from the local grocery and toss on a variety of favorite toppings to make it special. Try crumbled blue or feta cheese, freshly chopped herbs, sweetened dried cranberries, apple or avocado slices and walnuts...yum!

An Old-Fashioned
PICNIC

Mother's Cucumber Salad

Amy Gerhart
Farmington, MI

This is my mother's recipe...it always reminds me of summer and picnics. Cool, crisp, not to mention delicious, it tastes even better the longer it marinates in the refrigerator.

3 to 4 cucumbers, peeled and
    thinly sliced
3 T. salt
2 t. sugar
1/2 t. onion powder

1/4 t. celery seed
1/4 t. pepper
1/4 c. cider vinegar
Optional: 1/2 c. sliced red onion

Place cucumbers in a large bowl; add salt and enough water to cover. Cover and shake to mix salt. Refrigerate several hours to overnight. Drain cucumbers, but do not rinse; return to bowl. Stir together sugar, onion powder, celery seed, pepper and vinegar; mix well. Pour vinegar mixture over top of cucumbers. Add onion, if desired. Cover and shake gently to mix. Serves 6.

Tote a picnic lunch in style...in a one-of-a-kind bicycle basket! It's easy to make using a lidded craft-store container or a paper maché box. Simply attach stickers, glue on ribbon or decorate the container with acrylic paints. When the basket is done, punch holes in the back, thread lengths of ribbon through the holes and tie onto the handlebars with bows.

Sweet Beans

Sunshine Clark
Mill Creek, IN

Baked beans are an absolute summer picnic must-have. And with this very easy slow-cooker recipe, I don't even drain the beans.

1 lb. ground beef
1/2 lb. bacon, chopped
16-oz. can pork & beans
15-1/2-oz. can kidney beans
14-1/2-oz. can lima beans
1/2 c. brown sugar, packed

1/2 c. catsup
2 t. dry mustard
2 t. vinegar
1 t. salt
1/2 t. pepper

Brown ground beef and bacon in a large skillet over medium heat; drain. Add remaining ingredients; mix well. Pour into a lightly greased slow cooker. Cover and cook on low setting for 4 to 5 hours, stirring occasionally. Serves 4 to 6.

Pack a pair of whimsical salt & pepper shakers in the picnic basket. With so many clever designs, from hens & chicks to dancing veggies, they're can't-miss fun!

8 Great Burgers

Susie Backus
Gooseberry Patch

When there's a family picnic, I make sure the cooler and picnic basket are filled with all we need for these burgers...our kids named them and they're a hit. We have such fun with family gathered together...a special time for making memories.

1-lb. pkg. ground pork sausage
1-lb. pkg. ground beef
2 T. Worcestershire sauce
1/2 c. grated Parmesan cheese

1/3 t. pepper
8 hamburger buns, split
Garnish: lettuce, sliced tomato,
   sliced onion

Combine first 5 ingredients in a large bowl. Mix well; form into 8 patties. Grill burgers to desired doneness, about 5 to 6 minutes per side. Serve on buns with favorite toppings. Makes 8 servings.

Remember the great metal lunchboxes kids used to carry to school? Snap 'em up at flea markets...they bring back such sweet memories and are super for packing with picnic goodies.

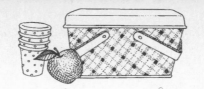

Grand Ma-Ma's Deviled Eggs

*Maureen Gillet
Manalapan, NJ*

This recipe, which was handed down to me over 30 years ago, is in memory of my very special mother-in-law, Charlotte. She was affection- ately named Grand Ma-Ma to all and her deviled eggs were always a hit with young & old alike.

4 eggs, hard-boiled, peeled
   and halved
1-1/2 t. vinegar
1/2 t. dry mustard
1/4 t. salt

1/8 t. pepper
1/2 t. sugar
1-1/2 T. butter, melted
1/4 t. Worcestershire sauce
Garnish: paprika

Scoop egg yolks into a bowl. Arrange egg whites on a serving platter; set aside. Mash yolks well with a fork. Add remaining ingredients except paprika; mix well. Spoon into egg whites; sprinkle with paprika. Makes 8 servings.

How do you like to go up in a swing,
Up in the air so blue?
Oh, I do think it is the pleasantest thing
Ever a child can do!
-Robert Louis Stevenson

E-Z Pickled Beets & Eggs

Pamela Berry
Huntington, IN

My mom and grandma always made pickled beets the old-fashioned way. Yes, they were delicious, but I was looking for a quick & easy way to prepare them...here's my secret!

12 eggs, hard-boiled and peeled

2 16-oz. jars sliced pickled beets

Place eggs in a large container. Pour beets and liquid over eggs. Cover and refrigerate for 2 to 3 days. Makes one dozen servings.

Shortcut to Grandma's Pickles

Melanie Lowe
Dover, DE

Fuss-free and packed with flavor.

4 Kirby cucumbers, quartered length-wise
2 to 3 sprigs fresh tarragon
1-3/4 c. white vinegar

1/3 c. sugar
1/4 t. red pepper flakes
1-1/2 t. coarse salt

Place cucumbers and tarragon in a large jar. Combine remaining ingredients in a saucepan over medium heat; cook and stir until sugar and salt are dissolved. Pour over cucumbers; cool completely uncovered. Refrigerate overnight before serving. May keep refrigerated up to 6 weeks. Makes 16 servings.

July is National Pickle Month...try whipping up a batch!

Michele's Fruit Sticks

Michele Pappagallo
London, AR

Years ago, I needed a quick recipe for a family picnic. After running out of ideas, I tossed these together, and they were a hit! So simple, and yet so good, they're a refreshing snack everyone loves.

1 c. orange segments
1 c. seedless green grapes
1 c. seedless red grapes
1 c. watermelon, cubed
1 c. cantaloupe, cubed

1 c. honeydew, cubed
1/2 c. maraschino cherries, drained
6 to 8 wooden skewers
crushed ice

Thread fruit onto extra-long bamboo skewers, leaving bottom 2 to 3 inches of each skewer unfilled. Fill a large serving bowl with crushed ice, and insert the bottom of each stick into crushed ice. Makes 6 to 8 servings.

A yummy fruit dip is perfect pairing with the sweet fruits of summer. Simply blend together 7 tablespoons marshmallow cream, 5 tablespoons softened whipped cream cheese and 3 to 4 tablespoons sour cream.

Perfect Picnic Pineapple

Dawn Psik
Aliquippa, PA

This dish is easy to make and so tasty. It whips up
in a jiffy and is great for a picnic.

20-oz. can crushed pineapple
1/2 c. sugar
2 eggs, beaten
1/2 c. cold water
2 T. cornstarch

1/2 t. vanilla extract
2 T. butter, diced
1 t. cinnamon

Combine pineapple with juice, sugar, eggs, water, cornstarch and vanilla in a medium bowl; mix well. Pour into a greased 9"x9" baking pan. Dot top with butter; sprinkle with cinnamon. Bake, uncovered, at 350 degrees for one hour. Makes 4 servings.

Fresh berries are plentiful in the summer...use them to top cupcakes, or serve sliced over vanilla yogurt. Share a pretty pint basket with neighbors...sure to bring a smile!

Sandy's Chicken-Rice Bake

Sandy Selfridge
Butler, PA

When I needed to make a dish for a summer picnic,
this is what I created...everyone loved it!

2-1/2 c. cooked rice
2 boneless, skinless chicken
   breasts, cooked and shredded
2 10-3/4 oz. cans cream of
   chicken soup

3/4 c. water
1 to 1-1/2 c. favorite shredded
   cheese

Spread rice in a lightly greased 13"x9" baking pan. Combine chicken, soup and water; mix well. Spread over rice; sprinkle with cheese. Bake, uncovered, at 350 degrees for 30 minutes, or until cheese is golden and bubbly. Serves 6.

Need a quick & easy side dish for Sunday dinner? Boil baby Yukon gold potatoes whole...no need to cut or peel. Then mash boiled potatoes with milk, butter and ricotta cheese to taste.

Sunbonnet Casserole

Jennifer Eveland-Kupp
Blandon, PA

I love this very easy and delicious casserole.

8-oz. pkg. medium egg noodles
4 eggs, hard-boiled, peeled and
   diced
10-3/4 oz. can cream of celery
   soup

1/2 c. milk
1/4 c. green pepper, chopped
2 T. onion, chopped
1 T. pimento, chopped
1/4 c. bread crumbs

Reserve half the noodles for another recipe. Cook remaining noodles according to package directions. Combine all ingredients except bread crumbs in a large bowl; fold in noodles. Pour into a lightly greased one-quart casserole dish; sprinkle with bread crumbs. Bake, uncovered, at 350 degrees for 20 minutes, or until golden. Serves 4 to 6.

Painting a watering can is a fast way to spruce it up for summer.
Coat the watering can with a primer made for metal and let dry.
Brush on latex paint, let dry, then seal with water-based
polyurethane. It's so easy!

Chicken Basket

Pat Akers
Bayfield, CO

A wonderful picnic food and goes so nicely with coleslaw and potato salad. Easy to carry to a picnic...wrapped in layers of newspaper, this little "basket" will keep warm until you reach your destination.

1/2 c. all-purpose flour	1 t. pepper
1-1/2 T. sesame seed	2 egg whites, beaten
1/2 T. poppy seed	8 chicken thighs or breasts
1/2 T. dried thyme	2 T. butter
3/4 t. dried tarragon	2 T. margarine
1 t. salt	1 loaf round sourdough bread

Combine flour, seeds and seasonings in a shallow bowl. Place egg whites in a separate shallow bowl. Dip chicken in egg whites; coat thoroughly with flour mixture. Melt butter and margarine in a large skillet over medium heat. Brown chicken thoroughly, about 7 minutes per side. Transfer chicken to a lightly greased 3-quart casserole dish. Bake, uncovered, at 350 degrees for 20 minutes; turn chicken over and continue to bake for an additional 20 minutes. Remove from oven. Cut a circle in top of loaf; set aside. Scoop out inside of loaf, leaving a shell of about 3/4 inch bread. With a pastry brush, spread butter sauce over inside of loaf and reserved top. Place chicken inside bread "basket" and set on a baking sheet. Place top of loaf alongside on baking sheet. Bake for 20 minutes, uncovered. Remove from oven; replace top of loaf and wrap in several layers of newspaper to keep warm. Makes 4 to 6 servings.

Herb & Seed Butter Sauce:

1/4 c. margarine	1 T. dried thyme
3 T. sesame seed	1-1/2 t. dried tarragon
1 T. poppy seed	

Melt margarine in a small saucepan over low heat; stir in remaining ingredients.

An Old-Fashioned
PICNIC

Zesty Horseradish Coleslaw

Diana Strawbridge
Ashtabula, OH

My family loves horseradish, the spicier the better! We also love coleslaw, especially for summer cookouts. It just seemed natural to combine the two and it turned out to be one of our favorite warm-weather salads!

1/2 c. mayonnaise
1/2 c. mayonnaise-type salad
   dressing
2 T. prepared horseradish

1-1/2 t. white vinegar
1-1/2 t. dill weed
3-1/2 T. sugar
16-oz. pkg. coleslaw mix

Stir together all ingredients except coleslaw mix in a large bowl; mix well. Add coleslaw; stir to coat. Refrigerate at for least 2 hours before serving; stir well. Serves 8.

Dreamy, creamy floats! Place scoops of cookie dough ice cream into the bottom of large glasses, then fill each glass with cream soda.

Watermelon Lemonade

Sherry Calloway
Spencer, IN

My family loves melon and this is a wonderful way to serve it on those hot summer days. The purée freezes well so this can be enjoyed in the winter months when you're missing summer.

4 c. watermelon, chopped
1 c. sugar

1-1/2 c. lemon juice
6 c. cold water

Place watermelon in a blender; process until smooth and set aside. In a large pitcher, combine sugar and lemon juice; stir until sugar is dissolved. Stir in water. Add watermelon; mix well. Serve very cold; stir well before serving. Makes 8 to 10 servings.

Lemon Daisy

Cheri Emery
Quincy, IL

Great on a warm summer day!

1/2 c. grenadine syrup
1/3 c. lemon juice

2 c. club soda, chilled
2 c. lemon-lime soda, chilled

Stir all ingredients together. Serve in ice-filled glasses. Makes 4 servings.

Picnics mean time for favorite games like hide & seek, water-filled squirt guns, kite flying...fun for kids of all ages. Top off the evening by roasting marshmallows.

An Old-Fashioned
PICNIC

Midwest Family Picnic Salad

Amy Barthelemy
Eagan, MN

You can also add diced ham, chicken or tuna...terrific!

16-oz. pkg. rotini pasta, cooked
15-oz. can pineapple tidbits,
   drained
1 c. seedless green grapes
1 c. seedless red grapes
1 c. green onions, chopped
1 c. celery, diced

2 carrots, peeled and grated
2 c. mayonnaise
14-oz. can sweetened
   condensed milk
1/4 c. sugar
1/2 c. vinegar

Combine pasta, fruit and vegetables in a large bowl; set aside. Mix together remaining ingredients until smooth. Add to pasta mixture, tossing to coat. Chill until serving time. Serves 12.

Slip bottles of water in the freezer...when frozen, pack inside the picnic cooler. They'll keep foods fresh and as they melt, you'll have lots of chilled water for quenching thirsts.

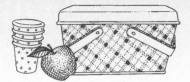

Mexican Burgers

Stacie Avner
Gooseberry Patch

One night our large family all wanted burgers, but disagreed on the type of burgers they wanted. So we made traditional cheeseburgers and these Mexican Burgers. When dinner was done, even the kids agreed these beat the cheeseburgers.

1 avocado, pitted, peeled
   and diced
1 plum tomato, diced
2 green onions, chopped
1 to 2 t. lime juice
1-1/4 lbs. ground beef
1 egg, beaten
3/4 c. to 1 c. nacho-flavored
   tortilla chips, crushed

1/4 c. fresh cilantro, chopped
1/2 t. chili powder
1/2 t. ground cumin
salt and pepper to taste
1-1/4 c. shredded Pepper Jack
   cheese
5 hamburger buns, split

Mix together avocado, tomato, onions and lime juice; mash slightly and set aside. Combine ground beef, egg, chips and seasonings in a large bowl. Form into 5 patties; grill over moderately high heat to desired doneness, turning to cook on both sides. Sprinkle cheese over burgers; grill until melted. Serve on buns; spread with avocado mixture. Makes 5.

Weathered, chippy pots are good buys at barn sales. Cleaned up
and dusted off, then filled with long-blooming annuals
like pansies or petunias, they're oh-so pretty!

An Old-Fashioned
PICNIC

Country Corn Salad

Kimberly Brindley
Woodbury, TN

A great barbecue or picnic side.

16-oz. pkg. frozen yellow corn,
   thawed and drained
1 green pepper, chopped
1/2 red onion, chopped
3 green onions, chopped

1-1/2 c. ranch salad dressing
2 to 3 T. bacon bits
1/2 t. cayenne pepper
salt and pepper to taste

Mix all ingredients together in a large bowl. Chill until ready to serve.
Serves 4 to 6.

A muffin tin makes a terrific condiment server. Fill each of the
cups with something different...relish, hot sauce, horseradish,
pickle slices, catsup and mustard are all ideal for
picnic sandwiches and burgers.

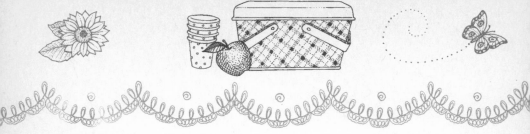

Grilled Cuban Sandwiches

Gladys Kielar
Perrysburg, OH

*A great combination of flavors...some Cuban sandwiches have layers
of thinly sliced cooked pork too. You can also grill sandwiches
on a countertop grill or a panini press.*

1 loaf French bread, halved
  lengthwise
2 T. Dijon mustard
6 ozs. Swiss cheese, thinly
  sliced

6 ozs. deli ham, sliced
8 dill pickle sandwich slices

Spread cut sides of bread with mustard. Arrange half each of cheese
and ham on bottom half of bread; top with pickle slices. Repeat
layering with remaining cheese and ham; cover with top half of bread.
Slice into quarters. Arrange sandwiches in a skillet that has been
sprayed with non-stick vegetable spray; place a heavy skillet on top
of sandwiches. Cook over medium-high for 2 minutes on each side,
or until golden and cheese is melted. Makes 4 servings.

A fast-fix veggie dip that's yummy! Stir together 1-1/4 cups sour cream
with 1/2 cup mayonnaise and a one-ounce package of dry onion soup
mix. Spoon dip into a serving bowl and garnish with minced chives.

Zesty Bean Salsa

Lori Rosenberg
Cleveland, OH

Great for picnics or community meals,
definitely a different twist on salsa.

1/2 c. oil
1/4 c. cider vinegar
1/4 c. sugar
1 green pepper, chopped
1 orange pepper, chopped
1 yellow pepper, chopped
1 red onion, chopped
4 stalks celery, chopped
16-oz. can black-eyed peas,
　　drained and rinsed

15-1/2 oz. can Great Northern
　　beans, drained and rinsed
15-oz. can shoepeg corn,
　　drained
7-oz. can chopped jalapeños,
　　drained, to taste
tortilla chips

Combine oil, vinegar and sugar in a saucepan over medium heat. Bring to a boil; set aside. Stir together remaining ingredients except tortilla chips in a large bowl. Drizzle with oil mixture to taste. Serve with tortilla chips. Makes 25 to 30 servings.

Salsa totes easily in a Mason jar...set a few varieties in a
milk bottle carrier for easy toting to any get-together.

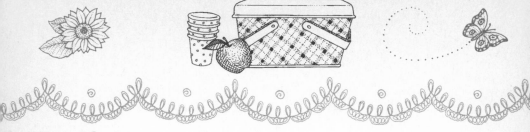

Ham & Macaroni Picnic Salad

Sandy Rowe
Bellevue, OH

*So easy and yummy...homemade really is better than store-bought,
and easier to prepare than you might think.*

16-oz. pkg. elbow macaroni,
  cooked
1 c. cooked ham, diced
1 c. celery, sliced
1/2 c. green onions, chopped
1/4 c. sweet pickle relish
2-oz. jar diced pimentos,
  drained

1 c. mayonnaise-type salad
  dressing
2 T. mustard
1/2 t. salt
1/4 t. pepper
4 eggs, hard-boiled, peeled and
  chopped

Combine macaroni, ham, celery, onion, pickle relish and pimentos; set aside. Combine remaining ingredients except eggs; blend well. Add to macaroni mixture; mix well. Gently stir in eggs. Serve immediately, or cover and refrigerate until serving time. Serves 8.

For a little extra sweetness, add a few orange slices to frosty,
ice-filled glasses before pouring in homemade lemonade.

An Old-Fashioned
PICNIC

Ada's Famous Broccoli Salad

Becky Jackson
Parkersburg, WV

My cousin Ada gave me this recipe. She brings it to all of our family's summer picnics and church dinners and it always disappears quickly!

1 lb. bacon, crisply cooked and
    crumbled
4 bunches broccoli, chopped
1 red onion, chopped
8-oz. pkg. shredded Cheddar
    cheese

1 c. mayonnaise
1 c. sugar
3 T. red wine vinegar

Toss together bacon, broccoli, onion and cheese in a large bowl; set aside. Combine remaining ingredients; mix well. Add to broccoli mixture; chill for 45 minutes before serving. Serves 8 to 10.

Keep salads chilled...simply nestle the salad serving bowl
into a larger bowl filled with crushed ice.

Picnic Barbecue Beans

Carol Hayden
Atwood, KS

This is a family favorite recipe that's been passed along to family & friends. Our potlucks and picnics are not complete without this dish!

4 slices bacon, chopped
1 yellow onion, coarsely
   chopped
4 14-1/2 oz. cans green beans,
   drained

1 c. catsup
1 c. brown sugar, packed

In a skillet over medium heat, cook bacon until crisp; remove bacon from skillet. Add onion to drippings in skillet; sauté until tender. Combine bacon, onion and remaining ingredients in a slow cooker; stir well. Cover and cook on low setting for 6 to 7 hours. Serves 10.

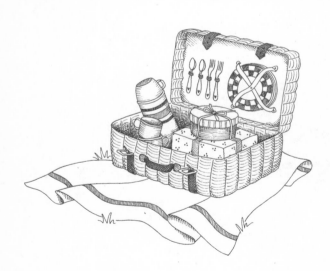

At the next tag sale, look for a vintage suitcase. Lined with pretty, new fabric and filled with picnic supplies, it's ready for a summer's day picnic whenever you are!

Mike's Grill Surprise

Amy Atkinson
Fowler, IN

*One of my husband's favorite foods from the garden is green beans.
So he combined his love of grilling, his favorite fresh vegetable and
a memory from his childhood to create this dish. What a great one-dish
summer meal!*

2 lbs. Polish sausage or pork
    tenderloin, cut into bite-size
    pieces
12-oz. can beer or non-alcoholic
    beer

6 to 8 new redskin potatoes,
    quartered
4 c. green beans, snapped
1 c. butter
salt and lemon pepper to taste

Combine all ingredients in a large disposable roaster. Add water to fill
1/4 of roaster. Cover with aluminum foil. Place roaster on a grill. Cook
over medium heat for 1-1/2 to 2 hours, checking after an hour and
adding more water if needed. Serves 6 to 8.

To keep tablecloths from blowing in the wind, gather the corners
below the table with gingham ribbon...picnic perfect!

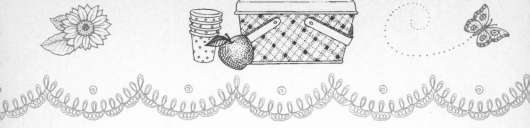

Homemade Potato Salad

Michelle Papp
Rutherford, NJ

*My Dad lives 3 hours away from me, so when I visit him for Fathers'
Day I fill a huge picnic basket filled with all of his favorites. Then I pack
a bag for the weekend and take off for a visit with the ingredients for a
good old-fashioned barbecue. This homemade potato salad is always on
the menu.*

2 lbs. redskin potatoes, boiled
  and sliced 1/2-inch thick
6 eggs, hard-boiled, peeled and
  chopped
1/4 c. red onion, chopped

2 stalks celery, chopped
8-oz. container sour cream
2 T. cider vinegar
1/4 c. mayonnaise

Combine potatoes, eggs, onion and celery in a large bowl; set aside. In
a separate bowl, mix sour cream, vinegar and mayonnaise together
until blended. Pour mixture over potatoes and toss to coat. Chill for at
least 2 hours before serving. Serves 6 to 8.

For a refreshing summertime treat, fill hollowed out
cantaloupe halves with vanilla ice cream...yummy!

An Old-Fashioned
PICNIC

Confetti Coleslaw

Dale Evans
Frankfort, MI

For an extra-special garnish, cut slits lengthwise in green onions and arrange on top of the coleslaw...mandarin oranges placed at the tip of each green onion will resemble a flower.

3 c. coleslaw mix
4 T. green onions, chopped and divided
1/4 c. red pepper, diced
1/4 c. green pepper, diced
3/4 c. frozen corn, cooked and drained

11-oz. can mandarin oranges, drained and divided
1/2 c. mayonnaise
2 T. sugar
1 T. raspberry vinegar
1 T. lime or lemon juice

Combine coleslaw mix, 3 tablespoons green onion, red and green pepper, corn and oranges, reserving 6 orange segments for garnish. Mix together mayonnaise, sugar, vinegar and juice; blend well. Pour over salad and toss to coat well. Garnish with remaining green onion and reserved orange segments. Transfer to a pretty serving dish. Serves 8.

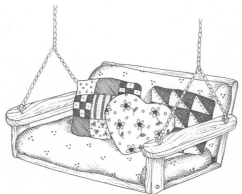

So clever...give a summertime bride & groom a picnic basket as a wedding gift. Filled with napkins, plates, flatware, glasses and gourmet goodies, a bow tied to the handle is all that's needed to top it off.

Grandmother's Garden Macaroni Salad

Sandy Carpenter
Washington, WV

My grandmother used to prepare this recipe when the whole family got together. We didn't live close, so when we'd visit, everyone would drop in. This salad brings back great memories whenever I put this on our table. We too, have moved away from family and it is a thrill when everyone visits.

8-oz. pkg. elbow macaroni, cooked
2 c. cooked ham, diced
1 c. Cheddar cheese, cubed
15-oz. can peas, drained
1 tomato, diced
1/2 c. green pepper, diced
1/4 c. onion, diced
1 t. salt
1/4 t. pepper
3/4 to 1 c. zesty Italian salad dressing

Combine all ingredients except salad dressing in a large bowl. Add dressing to taste, toss and refrigerate for about one hour before serving. Serves 6 to 8.

Save empty seed packets to make the sweetest magnets.
Cut a length of magnetic tape, peel the paper from the back
to reveal the sticky side and press to the back of a seed packet.

An Old-Fashioned
PICNIC

Summertime Pasta Salad

Crystal Kirby
Murfreesboro, TN

*This recipe is great for church picnics and potlucks. Not only is
it easy to prepare, but it can be tossed together the day before.
Everyone comes back for more...even the kiddies like it!*

13-1/4 oz. pkg. whole-wheat
  elbow macaroni, cooked,
  drained and cooled
1/2 c. green pepper, chopped
1/2 c. red pepper, chopped
10-oz. container grape tomatoes

3-1/2 oz. pkg. pepperoni,
  quartered
1/2 c. red onion, chopped
8-oz. pkg. Cheddar cheese cubes
16-oz. bottle Italian salad
  dressing

Mix all ingredients except salad dressing together in a large bowl with
a lid. Add salad dressing to taste; toss to mix well. Refrigerate for at
least 4 hours up to 24 hours, stirring or shaking occasionally. Keep
refrigerated until ready to serve. Makes 10 to 15 servings.

Slices of zucchini bread are scrumptious served alongside salads.
Cut shapes from softened butter with mini cookie cutters,
and place on a glazed new terra cotta saucer to serve.

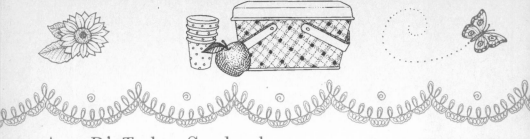

Aunt B's Turkey Sandwich

Bryna Dunlap
Muskogee, OK

This sandwich of mine is requested when we have our annual church picnic. For mini sandwiches, cut into even smaller slices.

1 c. sour cream
2 c. mayonnaise
2/3 c. green onions, chopped
2 t. chili powder
2 t. ground cumin
1 t. salt

4 loaves Italian bread, halved
  lengthwise
2 8-oz. pkgs. shredded Cheddar
  cheese
4 lbs. deli turkey, sliced
3 tomatoes, sliced

In a medium bowl, combine sour cream, mayonnaise, onions and seasonings. Spread over cut sides of bread. Layer bottom halves of bread with cheese, turkey and tomatoes; top with remaining bread. Slice each sandwich in half. Spray a griddle or large skillet with non-stick vegetable spray. Grill sandwiches for 5 minutes on each side, or until golden and cheese is melted. Slice into serving sizes. Makes 12 servings.

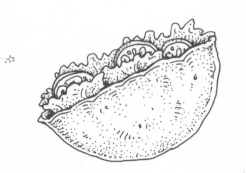

Put a new spin on picnic sandwiches by using different types of bread...herb loaves, French bread or focaccia. Split small rolls or stuffed pita bread sandwiches are easy for littler hands to hold.

Country-Style COOKOUT

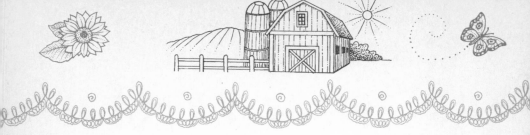

Cheeseburger Roll-Ups

Kelly Alderson
Erie, PA

*Made before we ever leave to go camping, these super-simple
sandwiches disappear just as soon as our tent is set up!*

2 lbs. ground beef
3/4 c. soft bread crumbs
1/2 c. onion, minced
2 eggs, beaten
1-1/2 t. salt
1-1/2 t. pepper

12-oz. pkg. shredded Cheddar
  cheese
6 to 8 sandwich buns, split
Garnish: catsup, mustard and
  lettuce

In a large bowl, combine beef, bread crumbs, onion, eggs, salt and
pepper; mix well. Pat out into an 18-inch by 14-inch rectangle on a
piece of wax paper. Spread cheese over meat, leaving a 3/4-inch
border around edges. Roll up jelly-roll fashion starting at short edge.
Press ends to seal. Place on a lightly greased 15"x10" jelly-roll pan.
Bake at 350 degrees for one hour, or until internal temperature on
a meat thermometer reaches 160 degrees. Let stand for at least
10 minutes before slicing. Slice and serve on buns; garnish as desired.
Serves 6 to 8.

No fire pit, no problem! Set up a portable camp stove on the porch
and pull out mini cast-iron skillets for the easiest of meals.
Whip up Italian sausages, fried new potatoes or
scrambled egg dishes...all in the great outdoors!

Granny's Campfire Special

Shelley Crook
Ellijay, GA

This is a recipe my grandmother made all of my childhood. In the beginning, she prepared it only when we would go camping, but we all loved it so much that she started serving it at home too. What's wonderful about this meal is that it's all in one pot and so easy to fix! Just serve it with cornbread or biscuits...sit back and watch everyone eat it up.

1 to 2 lbs. ground beef chuck
1 sweet onion, cut into rings
salt and pepper to taste
6 to 8 potatoes, peeled and
    thinly sliced

1 head cabbage, coarsely
    chopped
Optional: baby carrots

Crumble ground beef loosely in a Dutch oven. Lay onion rings over top; sprinkle with salt and pepper. Place potatoes in next; sprinkle with salt and pepper. Place cabbage over potatoes; top with carrots, if using. Cover and cook over medium heat for about 45 minutes, or until potatoes are tender. Serves 6.

One should learn also to enjoy the neighbor's garden,
however small; the roses straggling over the fence,
the scent of lilacs drifting across the road.

-Henry Van Dyke

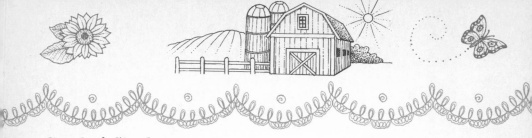

Sizzlin' Chicken

Donna Tennant
Jasper, IN

This chicken is a 4th of July favorite or, really, anytime favorite. The recipe has been in my family since I was a small child, and one of my fondest memories of summer is the aroma of this awesome chicken cooking on the grill.

2 T. garlic salt
1 t. onion salt
1 t. pepper
1 t. dried thyme

2 c. lemon juice
1 c. oil
2 to 3-lb. fryer chicken, cut into
    pieces

Mix seasonings together in a 2-gallon plastic zipping bag. Add lemon juice and oil. Seal bag; shake until mixed well. Add chicken; refrigerate for 8 hours, or overnight. Remove chicken from bag, discarding marinade. Place chicken on grill over low heat. Cook until chicken is done, watching very closely. Turn every 10 to 15 minutes, for 45 minutes to one hour. Makes 4 servings.

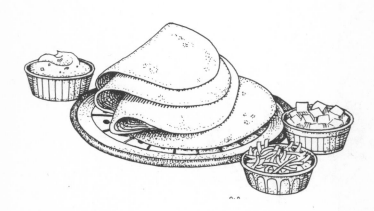

Leftover grilled chicken makes the best chicken fajitas
the next day! Simply heat and shred chicken,
fill tortillas and serve with salsa and guacamole.

Firecracker Grilled Salmon

Sharon Demers
Dolores, CO

*Add more red pepper flakes or a dusting of
cayenne pepper for even more heat!*

4 4 to 6-oz. salmon fillets
1/4 c. peanut oil
2 T. soy sauce
2 T. balsamic vinegar
2 T. green onions, chopped

1-1/2 t. brown sugar, packed
1 clove garlic, minced
1/2 t. red pepper flakes
1/2 t. sesame oil
1/8 t. salt

Place salmon in a glass baking dish. Whisk together remaining ingredients and pour over salmon. Cover with plastic wrap; refrigerate for 4 to 6 hours. Remove salmon, discarding marinade. Place on an aluminum foil-lined grill that has been sprayed with non-stick vegetable spray. Grill for 10 minutes per inch of thickness, measured at thickest part, until fish flakes when tested with a fork. Turn halfway through cooking. Serves 4.

Set up a table in a shady spot and load it up with a variety of
barbecue sauces, spreads, condiments, seasonings, all types
of breads, buns and rolls. Friends can pick and choose their
favorite combinations, or even try something new.

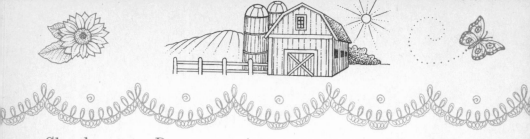

Chuckwagon Dogs

Dana Thompson
Gooseberry Patch

We made these on a whim one night while sitting around the backyard campfire. The kids loved them...and so did we!

16-oz. pkg. hot dogs
5 to 6 slices American cheese,
   sliced into 1/2-inch strips

12-oz. pkg. bacon

Split hot dogs without slicing all the way through. Place cheese strips down center of hot dogs. Wrap each hot dog with a slice of bacon; fasten with toothpicks. Roast over an open flame or hot coals until bacon is crisp-tender and hot dogs are heated through. Makes 10.

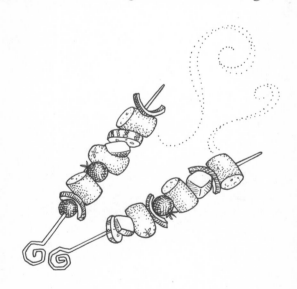

For a quick-fix cookout, slide precooked veggies and fully cooked
and sliced bratwurst or Italian sausage on metal skewers.
Grill kabobs over medium coals until heated through.

Country-Style
COOKOUT

Hank's Hot Sauce

Alysson Marshall
Newark, NY

This is my grandpa's recipe that has been handed down to my dad and now to me. It has a nice flavor for hot dogs and hamburgers, and isn't extremely spicy.

1 lb. ground beef	1 T. allspice
1 T. Worcestershire sauce	1/2 T. cayenne
1 T. chili powder	1 t. garlic salt
1 T. paprika	1 t. onion salt

Place ground beef in a medium saucepan; add water to cover meat. Add remaining ingredients; bring to a boil over medium heat. Reduce heat; simmer for about one hour, stirring occasionally to break up meat. Makes 3 cups and serves 12 to 15.

Dinners in a foil packet go hand-in-hand with any cookout. Combine potato and onion slices with a dash of paprika, garlic salt and pepper; drizzle with olive oil. Place in a square of heavy-duty aluminum foil, bring edges together to seal. Grill over medium heat for 25 minutes, or until potatoes are tender. Top servings with a dollop of sour cream and snipped chives. Yum!

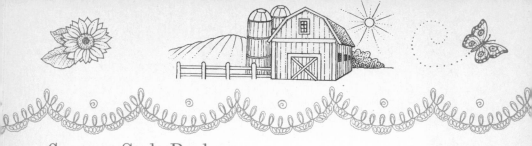

Country-Style Reuben

Jennie Gist
Gooseberry Patch

Piled high with corned beef and Swiss cheese, these pie iron sandwiches are so good you'll be making them all the time!

2 slices rye bread
2 t. butter, softened
1 slice Swiss cheese
2 to 3 slices deli corned beef

2 to 3 T. sauerkraut, drained
1 to 2 T. Thousand Island salad
   dressing

Butter one side of each bread slice. Place bread butter-side down into each side of pie iron. Layer remaining ingredients on one bread slice; carefully close pie iron. Grill over coals for 3 to 5 minutes on each side. Makes one sandwich.

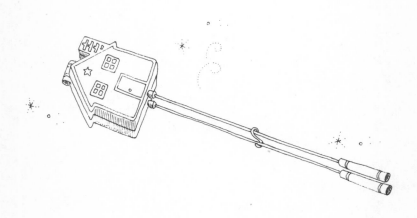

Pie irons make terrific cookout take-alongs. Available in round, square, rectangle or even hot-dog shapes, there's one for every favorite recipe!

Jalapeño-Bacon Cheese Steak

Lisa Robason
Corpus Christi, TX

Perfect for summertime grilling! We serve it with
borracho beans, Spanish rice and cornbread.

2 lbs. ground beef chuck
1-3/4 c. soft bread crumbs
3/4 c. beef broth
2 eggs, beaten
1 T. salt
1-1/2 t. pepper

8-oz. pkg. shredded Cheddar
  cheese
8 slices bacon, diced and
  crisply cooked
4 green onions, sliced
2 jalapeño peppers, diced

Place ground beef in a large bowl. In a separate bowl, mix bread crumbs and broth until thoroughly combined. Add bread mixture, eggs, salt and pepper to ground chuck; combine gently. Form into 8 patties. Grill over medium heat for about 8 minutes on each side, or place on a baking sheet and bake at 300 degrees for 30 minutes. Top with cheese, bacon, onions and peppers during the last few minutes of cooking. Makes 8 servings.

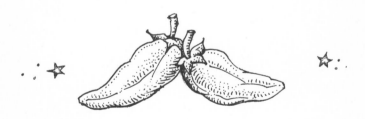

Garden-fresh herbs make the best butter. Blend together 1/2 cup butter with 1/2 cup shredded Cheddar cheese and 3 tablespoons chopped chives. Spread over grilled veggies or rolls, this butter is simply delicious!

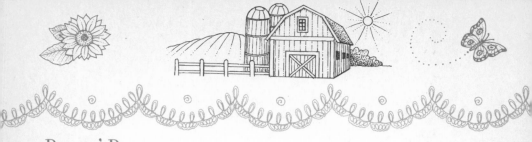

Poppin' Popcorn

Laura Fuller
Fort Wayne, IN

Our family has a fun song we always sing about popcorn popping on the apricot tree...the kids always think the white tree blossoms look like popcorn. Anyway, when it's time to sing this song, it's time to make this popcorn! We even planted popcorn that grew in our family garden last summer...what fun!

4 T. oil, divided
4 T. popcorn, unpopped
4 12" sqs. heavy-duty
   aluminum foil

4 T. butter, melted
salt to taste

Place one tablespoon oil and one tablespoon unpopped popcorn in the center of each aluminum foil square. Gather corners to form pouches. With string, tie corners of each pouch to roasting sticks. Place pouches directly on hot coals and shake often until corn is popped. Carefully open pouches and season to taste with butter and salt. Serves 4.

To add a new flavor to popped popcorn sprinkle on grated Parmesan cheese, ranch salad dressing mix or cinnamon-sugar.

Country-Style
COOKOUT

Salty & Sweet Snack Mix

Flo Burtnett
Gage, OK

*Whether it's a backyard campout or a camping vacation,
a snack mix is a must-have take-along treat!*

12-oz. pkg. bite-size crispy corn cereal
10-oz. pkg. doughnut-shaped oat cereal
10-oz. pkg. honeycomb-shaped corn & oat cereal
10-oz. pkg. mini pretzel twists
3/4 c. sugar
1/2 c. oil
1/4 c. margarine, melted
3 T. soy sauce
2 T. garlic salt

In a large bowl, combine cereals and pretzels. In a separate bowl, combine remaining ingredients; stir until sugar is dissolved. Pour over cereal mixture; toss until mixture is well coated. Transfer to a large ungreased roasting pan. Bake, uncovered, at 275 degrees for 1-1/4 hours, stirring every 15 minutes. Cool completely; store in an airtight container. Makes 10 quarts.

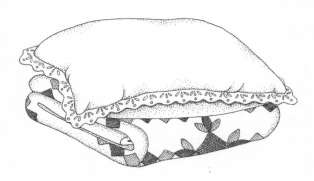

The relaxing scent of lavender is a simple country pleasure.
Hang a generous bouquet near towels and
sheets inside the linen closet.

Ribs with Espresso Barbecue Sauce

Jo Ann

*Ribs and barbecue sauce can be prepared one day ahead.
Just cool slightly, cover separately and refrigerate.*

2 T. hot Mexican-style chili
  powder
1 T. paprika
1 T. ground cumin
1-1/2 t. salt
3/4 t. pepper
4 lbs. baby back pork ribs, cut
  into serving-size pieces

12-oz. bottle dark beer
18-oz. bottle favorite barbecue
  sauce
1/2 c. water
2 T. brown sugar, packed
1 T. instant coffee granules

Whisk seasonings together in a small bowl to blend; rub mixture over ribs. Place ribs in a large heavy roasting pan. Bring beer to a boil over medium heat in a large saucepan; cook until reduced to one cup, about 5 minutes. Pour beer around ribs; cover tightly with aluminum foil. Bake at 400 degrees until fork-tender, about 1-1/2 hours. Combine remaining ingredients in a saucepan over medium heat. Simmer until slightly thickened, stirring occasionally, about 10 minutes. Brush ribs with barbecue sauce; grill on medium-hot coals for 3 minutes. Turn ribs; brush again with sauce and grill for an additional 3 to 4 minutes, until heated through. Bring remaining sauce to a boil; serve with ribs. Makes 4 to 6 servings.

Using jute, bundle fresh herbs together such as thyme,
sage or rosemary to create an herb basting brush...
it really adds flavor to grilled foods.

Carrie's Grilled Sweet Corn

Carrie Knotts
Kalispell, MT

To serve grilled corn, pull back the husks and tie with a piece of the husk to form a handle.

1/3 c. butter, softened
1-1/2 t. ground cumin
1-1/2 t. chili powder

2 cloves garlic, minced
12 ears sweet corn in husks

Blend together all ingredients except corn; chill. Cover corn with water; soak for 20 minutes. Gently pull back corn husks, leaving bases attached; remove silk and pat dry. Spread about one teaspoon butter over each ear of corn. Press husks back into place; tie with wet kitchen string. Place on grill over medium-high heat; close lid and cook, turning frequently, for about 20 minutes, or until husks are blackened and corn is tender. Makes one dozen servings.

Try spreading grilled sweet corn with softened butter that's been blended with fresh snipped marjoram or thyme, finely chopped shallots or minced garlic.

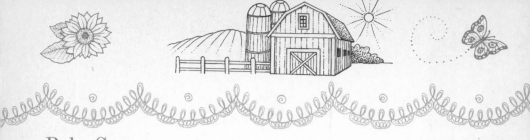

Ruby Sauce

Jill Valentine
Jackson, TN

Sweet, tart and absolutely the best sauce...you really have to try it on ribs, chicken or pulled pork!

1 c. brown sugar, packed
1 c. sugar
1 c. cider vinegar
1 t. ground ginger
1 t. cinnamon
1 t. allspice
1 t. paprika

1/2 t. ground cloves
1/2 t. red pepper flakes
1/2 t. salt
1/8 t. pepper
2 onions, finely chopped
4 c. rhubarb, finely chopped

Combine all ingredients except onions and rhubarb in a large saucepan over medium heat. Bring to a simmer; stir in onions and rhubarb. Cook for 45 minutes to one hour, until thickened and rhubarb is tender. Serves 4 to 6.

A backyard campout is a fun summertime get-together for kids...
staple a bag of mini marshmallows or trail mix to invitations!
Fun activities like a scavenger hunt, shadow puppets,
a nighttime flashlight walk and stargazing will be
sure to keep the fun going all evening long.

Country-Style
COOKOUT

All-American Summer Slaw

Julie Horn
Chrisney, IN

With no mayonnaise, this is a great salad to take camping and boating. We love it and it is very popular every time I make it.

16-oz. pkg. coleslaw mix
1/2 c. almonds, toasted
1-1/2 c. sweetened dried
   cranberries
1/2 c. celery, diced

1/4 c. green onions, sliced
1/2 c. green pepper, diced
1 c. honey mustard salad
   dressing

Combine all ingredients except salad dressing in a large bowl; mix well. Pour dressing over slaw mixture; stir well. Refrigerate until ready to serve. Mix well before serving. Serves 4 to 6.

Put streamers on bikes and flags on tricycles...summer's
the time for a backyard bike parade!

Tomato-Mushroom Grilled Fish

*Sharon Demers
Dolores, CO*

*This is a wonderful recipe for the summer months, and baking
in parchment paper or foil packets makes clean-up a breeze.
You can use orange roughy, sea bass or halibut.*

1 T. butter, softened
4 c. baby spinach
2 6-oz. white fish fillets,
    1/2-inch thick
salt and pepper
1/2 c. zucchini, cut into thin
    slivers

4 mushrooms, sliced
1 tomato, chopped
1/4 c. fresh basil, chopped
2 T. lime juice
1 T. olive oil

For each packet, layer 3 sheets of parchment paper or two 15-inch
pieces of aluminum foil. Spread butter down center of each piece. Lay
2 cups spinach on buttered area of each paper. Place fish on top;
sprinkle with salt and pepper to taste. Divide zucchini, mushrooms
and tomato evenly on top of fish. Sprinkle with basil, lime juice and
oil. To seal, fold one long edge of paper or foil over the other; tuck
short ends underneath. Be certain packets are tightly wrapped so
juices will not escape. Place on a baking sheet. Bake at 450 degrees
for 15 to 18 minutes, until fish flakes. When ready to serve, arrange
fish and vegetables on plates. Serves 2.

Arrange cushions on
hay bales for super easy,
country-style seating 'round
the campfire.

Herbed Shrimp Tacos

Lori Vincent
Alpine, UT

We love to make these tacos in the summer...we simply grill the shrimp on metal skewers after marinating. They're so good!

juice of 1 lime
1/2 c. plus 1 T. fresh cilantro,
   chopped and divided
1 t. salt
1/2 t. pepper
1/8 t. dried thyme
1/8 t. dried oregano
1 lb. uncooked medium shrimp,
   peeled and cleaned

1/2 c. radishes, shredded
1/2 c. green cabbage, shredded
1/2 c. red onion, chopped
Optional: 2 T. oil
10 6-inch flour tortillas,
   warmed

Combine lime juice, one tablespoon cilantro, salt, pepper and herbs in a large plastic zipping bag; mix well. Add shrimp; refrigerate for at least 4 hours. Mix together radish, cabbage, onion and remaining cilantro; set aside. Thread shrimp onto skewers; grill on a medium-hot grill until pink and cooked through, or, heat oil in a skillet over medium heat; sauté shrimp until done. Spoon into warm tortillas; garnish with guacamole and cabbage mixture. Makes 10 servings.

Guacamole:

2 avocados, pitted, peeled and
   mashed
1 T. sour cream
1 T. hot sauce

juice of 1 lime
1 t. garlic salt
1/4 t. pepper

Combine all ingredients in a small bowl.

Set citronella candles inside Mason jars and terra cotta pots & saucers...sure to keep the pesky pests away with summertime style!

Granny White's Barbecue Sauce

Vici Randolph
Gaffney, SC

*This recipe is one that my grandmother passed on to my mother
and me...it's so good over chicken or pork.*

1/2 c. margarine	3 T. sugar
3/4 c. onion, chopped	3 T. mustard
3/4 c. catsup	3 T. Worcestershire sauce
3/4 c. water	2 t. salt
1/3 c. lemon juice	1/2 t. pepper

In a skillet, melt margarine over medium heat; add onion. Cook
until soft and translucent. Add remaining ingredients; simmer for
15 minutes. Makes about 3-1/2 cups.

Sweet & Easy Salmon

Stephanie King
Richmond, KY

*This is a recipe my mother-in-law shared with me. So easy...simple
to whip up, short marinating time and a quick grill time.*

2 T. butter	2 t. soy sauce
2 T. brown sugar, packed	1/2 t. pepper
1 to 2 cloves garlic, minced	4 salmon fillets
1 T. lemon juice	

Combine all ingredients except salmon fillets in a small saucepan.
Cook and stir over medium until sugar is dissolved; cool. Place fillets
in a lightly greased 13"x9" baking pan; pour cooled marinade over
top. Let stand for 10 to 15 minutes. Remove salmon from baking
pan. Spray grill with non-stick vegetable spray and grill over hot coals
for 4 to 5 minutes on each side, basting occasionally with marinade.
Discard any remaining marinade. Serves 4.

Country-Style
COOKOUT

Sisler Family Spinach Hamburgers

Charlotte Keul
Des Moines, IA

This recipe has been passed down from my grandmother's family, and was a tradition in my home growing up. Now, I serve it to my family. A requested dish at all of our gatherings, we enjoy corn on the cob and macaroni salad with these burgers.

2 lbs. ground beef
10-oz. pkg. frozen chopped
   spinach, thawed
1/2 to 3/4 c. grated Parmesan
   cheese

1.35-oz. pkg. onion soup mix
4 to 6 sandwich buns, split

In a large bowl, combine all ingredients except buns, mixing well with hands. Form into 4 to 6 patties. Grill on a hot grill to desired doneness. Serve on buns. Makes 4 to 6 servings.

For the juiciest foods, flip grilled burgers with a spatula,
turn steaks or chicken with tongs, not a fork. The
holes a fork makes will let the juices escape.

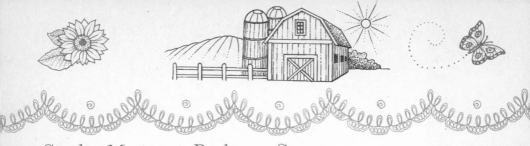

Smoky Mountain Barbecue Sauce

Toni Currin
Dillon, SC

Great on chicken...just add corn on the cob and your meal is complete!

1/4 c. oil
1/2 c. onion, chopped
1 clove garlic, minced
1 c. tomato purée
1 c. water

1 bay leaf, crushed
3 whole cloves
1 T. chili powder
1/4 c. brown sugar, packed
1/4 c. cider vinegar

Heat oil in a skillet over medium heat; add onion and garlic. Cook until onion is clear. Add remaining ingredients; simmer until sauce has thickened. Makes about 2-1/2 cups.

Cindy's Special Sauce

Cindy McKinnon
El Dorado, AR

My family loves this sauce...we always keep it on hand during the summer. It is so good on charcoal grilled burgers, hot dogs, fries and more!

1/4 c. butter
1 onion, chopped
24-oz. bottle catsup

1/2 c. white vinegar
3/4 c. brown sugar, packed

Melt butter in a saucepan over medium heat. Add onion and cook until onion is tender, about 5 minutes. Add remaining ingredients; simmer for 5 minutes. Makes 4 cups.

Bottle up sauces in glass jelly jars for gift giving
and add a calico topper...so pretty.

Grilled Potato Pouches

Cheri Emery
Quincy, IL

This is delicious no matter what's on the menu!

5 potatoes, peeled and sliced
1 onion, thinly sliced
6 T. butter
1 c. shredded Cheddar cheese
2 T. dried parsley

2 T. Worcestershire sauce
1/2 t. salt
1/4 t. pepper
1/3 c. chicken broth

Place potatoes and onion on a 22-inch by 18-inch piece of heavy-duty aluminum foil. Dot with butter. Sprinkle with cheese, parsley, sauce, salt and pepper. Fold up around potatoes; drizzle with broth. Seal well. Place on a hot grill for 35 minutes. Serves 6.

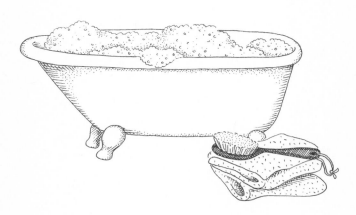

Tie together sprigs of fresh thyme, mint and tarragon with a
pretty ribbon. Hang the bouquet from the bathtub faucet
so that hot water splashes over it releasing its sweet
fragrance...an herbal home spa.

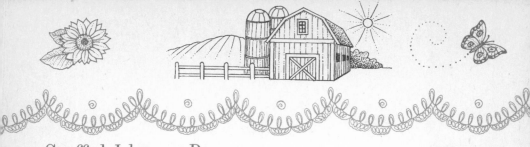

Stuffed Jalapeño Peppers

Lana Rulevish
Ashley, IL

It seems that anyone who likes spicy foods, loves these!

2 doz. jalapeño peppers
8-oz. pkg. shredded Mexican-
   blend cheese

1-lb. pkg. bacon, halved

Slice jalapeños lengthwise without cutting all the way through.
Remove seeds and veins. Stuff with cheese; close back up. Wrap a
half-slice of bacon around each jalapeño and secure with a toothpick.
Grill on each side for 2 or 3 minutes, until bacon is cooked and cheese
is melted. Makes 2 dozen.

Testing the heat on a charcoal grill or over a campfire is easy...
if you can hold your hand 5 inches over the coals for 2 to
3 seconds, the coals are hot; 4 to 5 seconds means the coals
are medium, and a full 6 seconds means the heat is low.

Savory Stuffed Potatoes

Betsy Ferris
Fultonville, NY

My father-in-law used to make these potatoes in the oven and serve them with London Broil. When my husband started grilling them for summer picnics, they quickly became a must-have.

6 baking potatoes
1 red onion, sliced
6 slices bacon, crisply cooked
   and crumbled
6 to 7 mushrooms, sliced

1/2 c. butter, thinly sliced
salt, pepper and garlic powder
   to taste
1 c. green onions, chopped
Garnish: fresh parsley sprigs

With a knife, make 4 to 5 cuts across each potato, without cutting through. Divide onion slices, mushrooms and bacon into slits of potatoes. Place butter slices in slits; sprinkle with salt, pepper and garlic powder. Top with green onion. Wrap each potato with aluminum foil; seal tightly. Place on a hot grill; cook until potatoes are tender. Garnish with parsley. Serves 6.

Share the garden's bounty when getting together for dinner with family & friends. Vintage fruit baskets found at a country flea market, lined with a tea towel or bandanna, are ideal for passing along prized tomatoes.

Topsy-Turvy Pizza

Ethel Kight
Moorefield, WV

We have enjoyed this recipe for years while traveling in our RV.

2 T. oil
1/2 lb. sweet or hot ground
   pork sausage
1 lb. ground beef
1 onion, chopped
3/4 t. garlic powder
3/4 t. Italian seasoning
14-1/2 oz. can pizza sauce

8-oz. pkg. shredded mozzarella
   cheese
1-1/2 c. all-purpose flour
1/4 t. salt
2 eggs, beaten
1 c. milk
1/2 c. grated Parmesan cheese

Heat oil over medium heat in a cast-iron skillet. Add sausage, ground beef and onion. Cook until browned; drain. Add garlic powder, Italian seasoning and pizza sauce; stir well. Sprinkle with mozzarella. In a large bowl, combine remaining ingredients except Parmesan; mix well. Spread over meat mixture; sprinkle with Parmesan cheese. Bake at 400 degrees for 20 to 30 minutes, or until golden. Makes 6 to 8 servings.

Keep summertime on-the-road meals easy with one-skillet
and one-pot recipes. Don't forget to pack a slow cooker
in the RV too...dinner will practically cook itself!

Country-Style
COOKOUT

Grilled Basil & Tomato Chicken

Vickie

A summertime favorite when spending time at the lake.

8 plum tomatoes, divided
3/4 c. balsamic vinegar
1/4 c. fresh basil
2 T. olive oil

1 clove garlic, minced
1/2 t. salt
4 boneless, skinless chicken
   breasts

Cut 4 tomatoes into quarters and place in a food processor; add vinegar, basil, oil, garlic and salt. Cover and process until smooth. Pour 1/2 cup of tomato mixture into a small bowl; cover and refrigerate until serving. Pour remaining tomato mixture into a large plastic zipping bag; add chicken. Seal bag; turn to coat. Refrigerate for one hour. Spray a grill rack with non-stick vegetable spray. Drain and discard marinade. Grill chicken, covered, over medium heat for 4 to 6 minutes on each side, or until juices run clear. Cut remaining tomatoes in half; grill for 2 to 3 minutes on each side, or until tender. Serve with chicken and reserved dressing. Serves 4.

For a perfectly patriotic 4th of July cookout, hang buntings
on the porch, fill vintage blue canning jars with white daisies
and tuck a flag bouquet into a watering can.

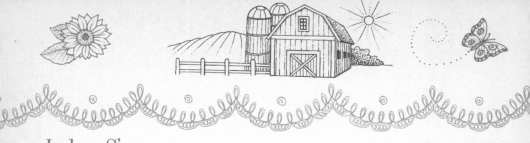

Indoor S'mores

Amy Hoover
Hampton, VA

I came up with this recipe in the summertime to use remaining marshmallows from winter's hot cocoa...it's a huge hit with friends!

12 whole graham crackers
1/4 c. butter
16-oz. pkg. marshmallows

12-oz. pkg. semi-sweet
   chocolate chips
1 c. chopped peanuts

Line a 15"x10" jelly-roll pan with aluminum foil; spray with non-stick vegetable spray. Arrange graham crackers in a single layer. Melt butter in a Dutch oven; add marshmallows, stirring constantly until melted. Place chocolate chips in a microwave-safe bowl; cook on high setting for 2 to 3 minutes, or until melted, stirring every 30 seconds. Add chocolate to marshmallow mixture. Stir to combine; immediately pour onto crackers and spread to edges. Sprinkle with chopped nuts. Cool until set, refrigerating if desired. Once cooled, remove mixture by lifting aluminum foil out of pan. With a pizza cutter, cut into 24 squares. Makes 2 dozen.

Toasted Taffy

Tina Wright
Atlanta, GA

One year at girls' camp we just had to have a sweet treat...these ingredients were on hand, and a new favorite was created!

12 caramels, unwrapped

24 round buttery crackers

For each, place a caramel on a long roasting stick. Hold over hot coals just until warm; place between 2 crackers, forming a sandwich. Makes one dozen.

Try making s'mores with chocolate graham crackers, toasted marshmallows and peanut butter cups...yummy!

Scrumptious Strawberry Kabobs

Sarah Hoechst
Bismarck, ND

An oh-so-easy way to enjoy sweet summer berries!

12 strawberries, hulled
12 doughnut holes
6 wooden skewers

1/4 c. semi-sweet chocolate
   chips
2 T. butter

Thread berries and doughnut holes alternately on skewers; place on a wax paper-lined baking sheet. In a small saucepan, combine chips and butter; melt over low heat, stirring until smooth. Drizzle over kabobs. Chill for 10 minutes, or until set. Makes 6 servings.

Grilled fruit is a great summertime dessert...try spooning
blueberries into pitted peach halves. Sprinkle on a little
brown sugar, wrap in aluminum foil and grill until
peaches are tender, about 10 minutes.

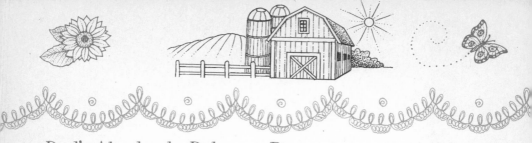

Dad's Absolutely Delicious Popcorn

Alissa Post
Scottsdale, AZ

This recipe was handed down to me from my dad...he is a wonderful cook! I have fond memories of helping him make batch after batch of this popcorn for church socials, church camping trips and family events.

1 c. butter
2 c. brown sugar, packed
1/2 c. light corn syrup
1 t. salt

1/2 t. baking soda
1 t. vanilla extract
6 qts. air-popped popcorn

Melt butter over medium heat in a saucepan; stir in brown sugar, corn syrup and salt. Bring mixture to a boil, stirring constantly. Boil without stirring for 5 minutes; remove from heat. Add baking soda and vanilla. Mix well and pour over popcorn; toss to mix well. Turn popcorn out onto 2 baking sheets that have been lightly sprayed with non-stick vegetable spray. Bake at 250 degrees for 15 minutes. Remove from oven and stir; bake for an additional 15 minutes. Cool; store in an airtight container. Makes 16 to 20 servings.

Save a corner in the garden to plant everlasting flowers such as strawflower, statice, globe amaranth, hydrangea and blue salvia. The flowers air dry beautifully and are oh-so pretty tucked into pails and baskets.

Country-Style
COOKOUT

Berry Cream Pie

Susanne Bennett
Northwood, NH

*Whether it's blueberry or raspberry, this pie recipe is a
family favorite for Memorial Day and 4th of July.*

3 c. blueberries or raspberries
9-inch pie crust
1 c. sugar
1/3 c. all-purpose flour

1/8 t. salt
2 eggs, beaten
1/2 c. sour cream

Place berries in unbaked pie crust; set aside. Combine sugar, flour and
salt. In a separate bowl, beat eggs and sour cream together; add to
flour mixture. Spoon over berries. Sprinkle topping over pie and bake
at 350 degrees for 50 to 55 minutes. Makes 6 to 8 servings.

Topping:

1/2 c. sugar
1/2 c. all-purpose flour

1/4 c. butter

Combine all ingredients until crumbly.

Sweet vintage pie plates can easily be found at barn sales and
flea markets. Words stamped inside like..."Flaky Crust" or
"Mellow Rich Pie" make them so charming. They're just
right for sharing a pie with a special friend.

Kathie's Packs-a-Punch Snack Mix

Kathie Lorenzini
Ignacio, CO

I like to take this on trips in the car...it provides lots of energy and is good for you too!

8-oz. pkg. fish-shaped pretzel crackers
1/2 c. whole almonds, toasted
1/2 c. hazelnuts, chopped
4-oz. pkg. dried blueberries
5-1/2 oz. pkg. dried cherries
1/2 c. sweetened dried cranberries
1/2 c. dried apricots, halved
1/2 c. chopped dates

Combine all ingredients in a large bowl. Store in an airtight container, or place in little snack-size containers for easy toting. Makes 24 servings.

When a snack mix recipe makes a lot of servings, spoon it into a nostalgic metal picnic tin along with a scoop. A stack of lunch-size paper bags nearby will make it easy for everyone to help themselves.

Fresh ...
From the
GARDEN

Summer Stuffed Tomatoes

Jennifer Oglesby
Brownsville, IN

This is actually my sister's recipe but it's so good that I had to share it! One of my favorite summer side dishes, these tomatoes are excellent with sweet corn fresh from your garden.

4 tomatoes
salt to taste
2-1/2 c. corn, divided
3 eggs, beaten

1/4 c. grated Parmesan cheese
1 T. fresh basil, finely chopped
salt and pepper to taste
4 slices provolone cheese

Cut 1/2-inch tops off tomatoes; scoop out insides. Lightly sprinkle insides of tomatoes with salt; turn tomatoes upside-down in a dish. In a food processor, purée 1-1/2 cups corn, eggs and Parmesan. Stir in remaining corn, basil, salt and pepper; mix well. Spoon into tomatoes; arrange in a lightly greased 9"x9" baking pan. Bake at 400 degrees for 40 minutes; place a cheese slice over each tomato and bake for an additional 5 minutes. Remove from oven and let stand for a few minutes before serving. Serves 4.

Add a whimsical scarecrow to a fence post...it's easy! Invert a sap bucket over the fence post, add a pole for arms, then dress him in a flannel shirt and stuff with straw. Paint a face on the sap bucket and top him off with a hat.

Fresh...From
THE GARDEN

Cheryl's Corn Fritters

Cheryl Lagler
Zionsville, PA

I generally don't get many of these fritters to the table for dinner since my kids (and I!) nibble on them as soon as they're done. Even when summer corn is gone, you can still have yummy corn fritters by substituting frozen corn.

2 c. corn
1 egg, beaten
1-1/2 t. sugar
2 T. butter, melted and divided

1/3 t. salt
1/8 t. pepper
1/4 c. all-purpose flour
1/2 t. baking powder

Combine corn, egg, sugar, one tablespoon butter, salt and pepper. Add flour and baking powder; mix well. Heat remaining butter in a medium skillet over medium-high heat; drop batter by 1/4 cupfuls. Cook for 2 to 3 minutes per side, or until golden. Serves 6.

Country Fried Green Tomatoes

Angie Stone
Argillite, KY

During the summer when green tomatoes are plentiful in our garden, everyone in my family enjoys these fried green tomatoes.

1 c. buttermilk
1 egg, beaten
1 c. cornmeal
1/2 c. all-purpose flour
2 T. sugar

1/8 t. salt
1/4 t. pepper
2 to 3 green tomatoes, sliced
    1/2-inch thick
oil for frying

Whisk together buttermilk and egg in a shallow bowl. Combine cornmeal, flour, sugar, salt and pepper. Dip tomato slices into buttermilk mixture; coat in cornmeal mixture. Heat oil, about one-inch deep, in a large skillet over medium-high heat. Cook tomatoes for 4 minutes on each side, or until golden. Serves 4.

Jalapeño-Cilantro Dressing

Lisa Langston
Conroe, TX

A dear friend shared this recipe with me...it's so delicious. Great as a salad dressing or as a dip with tortilla chips or vegetables.

1 bunch fresh cilantro
2 jalapeño peppers, seeded and
   minced
2 cloves garlic, minced

1/4 c. white wine vinegar
1/4 c. water
1 c. sour cream
1 c. mayonnaise

Place first 5 ingredients in food processor; process until well blended. Pour mixture into a bowl. Add sour cream and mayonnaise; stir to combine. Store in refrigerator for up to a week. Makes 2 cups.

Honey-Lime Dressing

Jennifer Eveland-Kupp
Blandon, PA

A sweet-tart flavor that will be a new favorite for your family.

1 c. sugar
1/2 c. honey
2 T. dry mustard
1 t. ground ginger

1/3 c. lime juice
1/3 c. water
2 c. corn oil

Process all ingredients except oil in a blender. Slowly add oil and continue to process until well blended. Store in refrigerator until ready to serve. Makes about 3 cups.

Serve up summer salad dressings in Mason jars with a vintage
serving spoon...a pretty country touch for any table.

Fresh...From
THE GARDEN

Tangy Watermelon Salad

Belva Conner
Hillsdale, IN

I won first prize at a Ladies' Day salad contest during our county fair. Everyone is surprised to see watermelon and onions together, but when they taste the salad they really like it, and always ask for the recipe.

14 c. watermelon, cubed
1 red onion, halved and thinly
   sliced
1 c. green onions, chopped
3/4 c. orange juice
5 T. red wine vinegar
2 T. plus 1-1/2 t. honey

1 T. green pepper, finely chopped
1/2 t. salt
1/4 t. pepper
1/4 t. garlic powder
1/4 t. onion powder
1/4 t. dry mustard
3/4 c. oil

In a large bowl, combine watermelon and onions; set aside. In a small bowl, combine orange juice, vinegar, honey, green pepper and seasonings; slowly whisk in oil. Pour over watermelon mixture; toss gently. Cover and refrigerate for at least 2 hours. Serve with a slotted spoon. Makes about 10 servings.

It's easy to cube a watermelon. Lay a few slices horizontally on
a cutting board and cut lengthwise. Next, turn the cutting
board and slice again to create cubes...so simple.

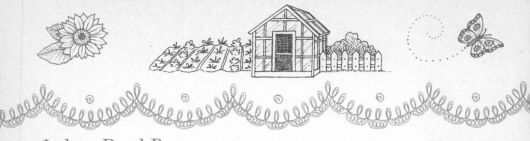

Italian Basil Pesto

Kay Barg
Sandy, UT

Pesto is delicious spread on a sandwich or layered with almost any appetizer dip. Try spreading it over any thin cut of meat or fish, then coat with bread crumbs and grill.

1 c. fresh basil
1 c. baby spinach
2 T. garlic, minced
1/4 c. pine nuts
1/4 c. grated Romano cheese

1/2 t. salt
1/4 t. pepper
1/2 c. olive oil
1/2 c. vegetable oil

In a food processor, combine all ingredients except oils. Pulse on and off 5 to 6 times to chop basil and spinach. With the motor running, add oils in a slow stream until creamy in texture. Makes about 2 cups.

Fresh basil makes the most delicious basil butter. Measure 1-1/2 cups packed leaves, then finely chop...kitchen scissors are great for this. Add basil to 2 cups softened butter; blend well. Basil butter is tasty on grilled foods or steamed veggies.

Greek Pizza

Dawn Horton
Columbus, OH

My husband and I love making this recipe in the summer. Every Saturday morning we go to the farmers' market to buy basil that's been freshly picked that same morning...a tradition we look forward to each summer.

1 c. basil pesto sauce
12-inch Italian pizza crust
1 c. shredded mozzarella cheese
1-1/2 c. cooked chicken, diced
1/2 c. red onion, chopped
1/2 c. green pepper, chopped
1/4 c. sliced black olives
Optional: 1/4 c. sliced banana peppers
4-oz. container crumbled feta cheese
1/8 t. dried oregano

Spread pesto on pizza crust; sprinkle with mozzarella cheese. Add remaining ingredients in order listed. Bake at 450 degrees for 10 minutes, until crust is golden and cheese has melted. Makes 6 to 8 servings.

If a recipe calls for just half of an onion, keep the remaining half fresh for another recipe. Rub the cut side with butter, place in a plastic zipping bag and refrigerate.

Cool Summer Squash Soup

Pamela Jones
Fredericksburg, VA

This soup is delicious served warm or cool. On a hot summer day, when appetites are small, this makes a perfect meal with a few extras such as bread sticks or French bread on the side. If you like, sprinkle shredded Parmesan cheese and croutons on top.

1 clove garlic, minced
1/4 c. olive oil
1 c. sweet onion, chopped
1 to 2 yellow squash, sliced
1 to 2 zucchini, sliced
16-oz. can diced tomatoes

Optional: 1/2 spaghetti squash
14-1/2 oz. can chicken or
   vegetable broth
1/4 t. dried oregano
1/4 t. dried parsley
salt and pepper to taste

In a large saucepan over medium heat, sauté garlic in oil. Remove garlic; add onion and squash. Sauté until soft. In a large soup pot, add squash mixture and remaining ingredients. Simmer for 30 minutes; cool. Refrigerate until ready to serve. Serves 4.

Spaghetti Squash Variation:

Microwave spaghetti squash on high setting cut-side down for 8 minutes, or until easy to remove. Remove seeds; with a fork, scrape out pulp which will resemble spaghetti. Cool; add pulp to soup mixture.

For savory soup croutons, heat one tablespoon olive oil in a large skillet. Add as much chopped thyme, oregano and tarragon as desired, then stir in 2 bread slices that have been cubed. Cook until lightly golden, then garnish soup servings.

Fresh...From
THE GARDEN

Mom's Squash Casserole

Cheryl Donnelly
Arvada, CO

Many years ago, my aunt gave this recipe to my mother. She often makes it in the summer to use the bounty of squash from her garden.

3 lbs. zucchini and/or yellow
   squash, sliced
1 onion, chopped
1 egg, beaten

salt to taste
1/2 c. butter, melted and divided
2 c. round buttery crackers,
   crushed

Cook squash in boiling water until tender; drain and mash. Add onion, egg, salt and half of melted butter. Pour mixture into a greased 13"x9" baking pan. Sprinkle with crushed crackers; drizzle with remaining butter. Bake, uncovered, at 350 degrees for one hour. Makes 10 to 12 servings.

Stuffed Pepper Wedges

Kathleen Felton
Fairfax, IA

These are a wonderful, easy-to-prepare appetizer. In summer, I make these quite often using red, yellow and green peppers fresh from my garden. They're so pretty, and a real crowd pleaser.

1/2 c. chive & onion cream
   cheese spread
1 T. chopped black olives

2 green, red or yellow peppers,
   sliced into 8 wedges
1/4 c. shredded Cheddar cheese

Mix cream cheese and olives together in a small bowl. Spread about 2 teaspoons of mixture on each pepper wedge; sprinkle with cheese. Arrange peppers on an aluminum foil-lined baking sheet. Broil in oven for 6 to 8 minutes, or until cheese is melted and peppers begin to char slightly. Serve warm or cold. Makes 16.

3-Cheese Pasta Bake

Marjorie Lischer
Longmont, CO

*One of those super-easy main dishes that's easy to
whip up and everyone loves!*

16-oz. pkg. frozen cheese
   ravioli or tortellini
2 T. butter
2 T. olive oil
1 red pepper, diced
1 green pepper, diced
salt and pepper

26-oz. jar spaghetti sauce
8-oz. pkg. shredded mozzarella
   cheese
1/4 c. shredded Asiago cheese
1/4 c. grated Parmesan cheese
1 T. dried oregano

Thaw ravioli or tortellini for 15 minutes. Melt butter and oil in a large
skillet over medium-high heat; sauté peppers for about 5 minutes,
until tender. Sprinkle with salt; set aside. Spread a thin layer of sauce
in an ungreased 13"x9" baking pan. Arrange half each of ravioli,
pepper mixture, cheeses and oregano; pour half of remaining sauce
over top. Repeat layering with remaining ingredients. Bake,
uncovered, at 375 degrees for 40 to 45 minutes, until bubbly and
golden. If the cheese begins to brown a little early, simply place
aluminum foil over the top of the dish as it continues baking. Serves
6 to 8.

A cool idea....a handy enamelware
pail makes an ideal ice bucket for
toting to the garden for summertime
weeding. Filled with bottles of water
or juice, it keeps thirst-quenching
cool drinks close at hand.

Fast-Fix Pasta Primavera

Deborah Clouser
Toccoa, GA

*This is the best of "fast food" at our house...we enjoy this
whenever we want a quick meal.*

3 c. combination of peas, green
   beans, broccoli, carrots and
   cauliflower, sliced or chopped
2 T. olive oil
16-oz. pkg. fettuccine pasta,
   uncooked

1/2 c. butter, sliced
1/2 to 1 c. grated Parmesan
   cheese
1 c. whipping cream
salt and pepper to taste

In a skillet over medium heat, sauté vegetables in oil until crisp-
tender. Cook pasta according to package directions; drain and return
to pot. Add butter to melt. Stir in sautéed vegetables and remaining
ingredients to pasta; mix well. Serves 6.

Line up a collection of folky birdhouses on a bench...sure to
bring a smile to anyone visiting a garden patch.

Old-Fashioned Switchel

Krysti Hilfiger
Covington, PA

This is truly an old recipe. Growing up with my grandmother on her farm, this is what she prepared for the men when it was hay season. It quenched their thirsts, but us kids liked to drink it "just because!"

8 c. cold water
1 c. sugar
1/3 c. cider vinegar

1 t. ground ginger
ice cubes

Mix all ingredients except ice cubes together in a large pitcher. Serve over ice in tall glasses. Makes 8 servings.

Lemon-Ginger Iced Tea

Angie Biggin
Lyons, IL

Lemon and ginger are a refreshing combination.
This tea goes well with any summer entrée or side dish.

4 c. water
1 lemon, halved
2 T. fresh ginger, peeled and grated

1/4 c. sugar
ice cubes
Garnish: 1 lemon, sliced

Bring water to a boil in a saucepan over medium-high heat. Halve one lemon; squeeze juice into pan. Stir in ginger; simmer for 15 minutes. Strain tea into a large pitcher; stir in sugar until dissolved. Refrigerate until well chilled. Pour tea into glasses over ice. Garnish with lemon slices. Serves 6.

Serve up icy drinks in frosty Mason jars...spritz with water,
then place in the freezer to frost.

Fresh...From
THE GARDEN

Lemon-Lime Slush

Angie Venable
Gooseberry Patch

Growing up, I remember summers at my grandmother's home. She was affectionately called "Mom" by everyone...her home was surrounded by fragrant lilacs, and beside the drive was a large vegetable garden. After a morning of weeding and picking vegetables, we'd come inside, sit in front of a fan and enjoy a tall glass of this frosty slush.

2 c. sugar
6 c. water, divided
1/4 c. fresh mint leaves
12-oz. can frozen orange juice
    concentrate

6-oz. can frozen lemonade
    concentrate
6 c. club soda, chilled

In a heavy saucepan, mix sugar, 3 cups water and mint leaves. Bring to a boil over medium-high heat; reduce heat and simmer for 2 minutes. Remove pan from heat; cool one hour. Strain mixture, discarding mint leaves. In a large non-metal freezer container, combine strained liquid, remaining water and juice concentrates; mix well. Cover and freeze until solid. To serve, scrape 2/3 cup slush mixture into a serving glass; slowly pour 1/3 cup club soda over slush. Makes 14 to 16 servings.

Wooden pop bottle crates are just right for storing summer plates, cups, flatware and other picnic must-haves.

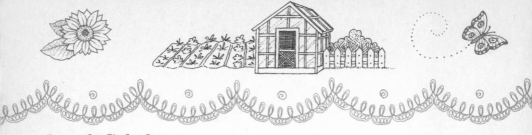

Israeli Salad

Carol Lowery
Eastman, GA

This recipe was given to me by friends from Colorado while they were staying at our horse farm. If you'd like, add olives, chickpeas, jalapeños and diced avocados. It can even be spooned into a pita pocket for easy serving.

2 to 4 cucumbers, diced
4 tomatoes, diced
1 green pepper, diced
1 red pepper, diced
1 onion, diced

2 c. canned corn
2 T. olive oil
1 t. salt
1 T. lemon juice

Combine all ingredients in a large bowl; mix well. Makes 6 to 8 servings.

Tuck a few lightweight sling or folding chairs in the trunk...
handy as extra seating for any outdoor get-together.

Scrumptious Summer Salad

Brenda Hughes
Houston, TX

A cool, fresh salad. Packed with flavor,
it's one salad that my family loves.

2 c. fresh or frozen corn, cooked
1 avocado, pitted, peeled and
  cubed

1 pt. cherry tomatoes, halved
1/2 c. red onion, finely diced

Combine all ingredients in a large bowl. Pour dressing over salad; toss gently to mix. Refrigerate until ready to serve. Serves 6.

Dressing:

2 T. olive oil
1 T. lime juice
1/2 t. lime zest

1/4 c. fresh cilantro, chopped
1/2 t. salt
1/2 t. pepper

Whisk together all ingredients in a small bowl.

Bring a little Texas to a summertime picnic! Fill Mason jars
with cool water and cheery sunflower bouquets...
a perfect fit tucked inside cowboy boots!

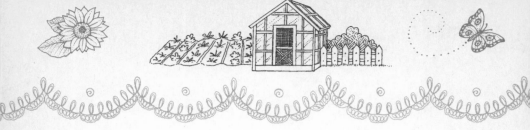

Texas-Style Cabbage

Janet Sue Burns
Granbury, TX

Topped with toasted almonds and a sprinkling of Parmesan cheese, this dish is great served with sliced corned beef and glazed carrots.

1/4 c. sliced almonds
1 head green cabbage, sliced
   1/2-inch thick
1/4 c. butter, sliced

1 clove garlic, minced
1 t. Italian seasoning
salt and pepper to taste
1/3 c. grated Parmesan cheese

Toast almonds in a medium skillet over low heat, stirring occasionally to prevent burning; set aside. Separate cabbage into strips; layer in skillet with butter, garlic and seasonings. Cook over medium-high heat until tender, stirring frequently. Garnish with cheese and toasted almonds. Serves 4 to 6.

A fresh tomato salad is a snap to prepare. Whisk together 1/4 cup white vinegar with one teaspoon chopped banana pepper and 3/4 teaspoon salt. Drizzle over one cup thinly sliced onion and 4 tomatoes cut into thin wedges. Let stand 15 minutes before serving.

Basil-Tomato Tart

Ann Fehr
Trappe, PA

A trip to the farmers' market means coming home with the freshest tomatoes and basil for this recipe. Not to mention, a lot of other wonderful fruits & veggies for your family to enjoy!

9-inch pie crust
1-1/2 c. shredded mozzarella
   cheese, divided
5 roma tomatoes, sliced into
   wedges
1 c. fresh basil

4 cloves garlic
1/2 c. mayonnaise
1/4 c. grated Parmesan cheese
1/8 t. white pepper
Optional: fresh basil leaves

Place pie crust in a 9" pie plate. Flute edge or press with the tines of a fork, if desired. Line crust with a double thickness of aluminum foil. Bake at 450 degrees for 8 minutes. Remove foil; bake for an additional 4 to 5 minutes. Remove from oven. Reduce temperature to 375 degrees. Sprinkle crust with 1/2 cup mozzarella cheese; cool on a wire rack. Arrange tomato wedges over melted cheese. In a food processor, combine basil and garlic; process until coarsely chopped. Sprinkle over tomatoes. In a medium bowl, combine remaining mozzarella cheese, mayonnaise, Parmesan cheese and pepper. Spoon evenly over basil mixture to cover top. Bake at 375 degrees for 35 to 40 minutes, or until top is golden and bubbly. Garnish with additional basil, if desired. Serve warm. Makes 6 servings.

Call friends and enjoy a summer's afternoon tea together. Use the pretty floral china you're saving for "someday" and spread an embroidered cloth on the table. Enjoy just being together!

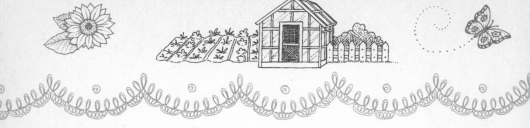

Stuffed Eggplant Boats

Michelle Papp
Rutherford, NJ

I just whipped this up one day in my kitchen!

2 eggplants, peeled and halved
   lengthwise
1 t. salt
2 potatoes, peeled and chopped
4 T. olive oil, divided
1 c. onion, diced

1 red pepper, diced
2 cloves garlic, minced
salt and pepper to taste
8-oz. pkg. shredded mozzarella
   cheese
1 c. dry bread crumbs

Scoop out the middles of eggplants to form boats. Lightly salt boats; spray with non-stick vegetable spray on all sides. Set aside on a greased baking sheet. In a skillet, cook potatoes in 3 tablespoons olive oil until golden. Remove with a slotted spoon to a separate plate. Add onion, pepper and garlic to skillet. Cook until onion is translucent and pepper is tender. Return potatoes to pan; sprinkle with salt and pepper to taste. Fill eggplant boats with mixture. Top with cheese and bread crumbs; drizzle with remaining oil. Bake at 350 degrees for 30 minutes, or until tender. Serve immediately. Serves 4.

Eggplants stay fresh just a few days, so it's best to keep them
stored in the crisper of the refrigerator, unwrapped. This way,
they'll be ready for any garden-fresh recipe for about one week.

Laurie's Stuffed Peppers

Laurie Patton
Pinckney, MI

*For this recipe, I like to use red, yellow and orange peppers
for a colorful, summertime look and sweeter taste.*

4 green, red or yellow peppers
2 T. olive oil
8-oz. pkg. mushrooms, finely
   chopped
1 onion, finely chopped
1 clove garlic, pressed
1 c. white rice, cooked

1 c. brown rice, cooked
3 to 4 dashes hot pepper sauce
salt and pepper
2 15-oz. cans tomato sauce,
   divided
1 c. shredded mozzarella cheese

Slice off tops of peppers; remove seeds. In a large soup pot, bring
water to a boil over medium-high heat. Add peppers; boil for
5 minutes. Remove peppers; set aside. Heat oil in a large skillet over
medium heat; add mushrooms, onion and garlic. Sauté for 5 minutes,
until onion is tender. Add rice, hot sauce, salt and pepper; cook for
2 minutes. Add one can tomato sauce and simmer for 5 minutes;
spoon into peppers. Spread 1/2 can tomato sauce into an ungreased
13"x9" baking pan. Place peppers in pan; pour remaining sauce over
top. Bake, uncovered, at 350 degrees for 25 minutes; sprinkle with
cheese. Bake for an additional 10 minutes, or until cheese is melted.
Serves 4.

Use dried herbs from the herb garden to make a terrific seasoning
blend. Combine one cup sea salt with 2 tablespoons each of
rosemary, thyme, lemon balm, mint, tarragon, dill weed and
paprika. Stir in 4 tablespoons parsley and basil. Blend, in
batches, in a food processor, and store in a glass shaker.

Dennis Family Broccoli Casserole

Lisa Burns
Findlay, OH

This is a family favorite that's easy to make...everyone enjoys it!

2 10-oz. pkgs. frozen chopped
  broccoli, cooked and drained
2 T. onion, grated
6-oz. pkg. herb-flavored
  stuffing mix

1/2 c. butter, melted
10-3/4 oz. can cream of chicken
  soup
10-3/4 oz. can cream of
  mushroom soup

Combine broccoli, onion and stuffing mix. Place in a lightly greased 2-quart casserole dish; drizzle with melted butter. Combine soups and spoon over broccoli mixture. Do not mix. Cover and bake at 350 degrees for 30 minutes. Remove cover and bake an additional 15 minutes. Serves 8.

This summer, clean house and host "the tag sale of the century!" Spread the word by placing an ad in the local paper and telling friends & neighbors. Have the kids set up a table that's filled with baked goodies and lemonade for sale.

Fresh...From
THE GARDEN

Skillet-Toasted Corn Salad

Sherri Cooper
Armada, MI

*Whenever my father comes to visit, this salad is one that he requests.
He usually stops by the local farmers' vegetable stand on his way to
our house and picks up fresh ears of corn...just for this salad!*

1/3 c. plus 1 T. olive oil, divided
1/3 c. lemon juice
1 T. Worcestershire sauce
3 cloves garlic, minced
3 to 4 dashes hot pepper sauce
1/4 t. salt
1/2 t. pepper
6 ears sweet corn, husked and
   kernels removed

4 red, yellow and/or green
   peppers, coarsely chopped
1/2 c. shredded Parmesan
   cheese
1 head romaine lettuce, cut
   crosswise into 1-inch pieces

In a jar with a tight-fitting lid, combine 1/3 cup oil, lemon juice,
Worcestershire sauce, garlic, hot sauce, salt and pepper. Cover and
shake well; set aside. Heat remaining oil in a large skillet over
medium-high heat. Add corn; sauté for 5 minutes, or until corn is
tender and golden, stirring often. Remove from heat; keep warm.
Combine corn, peppers and cheese in a large bowl. Pour dressing over
top; toss lightly to coat. Serve over lettuce. Makes 6 to 8 servings.

And when you want your dinner, don't buy it from a shelf,
You find a lettuce fresh with dew and pull it for yourself.
-Vintage Children's Reader

Mom's Yummy Cornbread Salad

Denise Neal
Castle Rock, CO

Because this salad disappears so quickly when I serve it at summer get-togethers, I usually double the recipe! Mom was a great cook, and it makes me feel close to her when I prepare her recipes. When I compiled a family cookbook recently, this recipe was a must-have.

1 c. cornbread, coarsely
  crumbled
8-3/4 oz. corn, drained
1/2 c. green onions, chopped
1/2 c. cucumber, chopped
1/2 c. broccoli, chopped
1/2 c. red pepper, chopped

1/2 c. tomato, chopped
1/2 c. canned pinto or garbanzo
  beans, drained and rinsed
1/2 c. shredded Cheddar cheese
1/2 c. buttermilk ranch salad
  dressing
salt and pepper to taste

Combine all ingredients in a large bowl, adding salt and pepper to taste. Gently mix and cover. Best when refrigerated for at least 4 hours before serving. Serves 6.

Keep a basket filled with flatware, napkins and acrylic dishes...
picnic perfect and ready at a moment's notice!

Tangy Tomato Aspic Salad

Bill Weedman, Jr.
Algoma, WI

We like to sprinkle a teaspoon of blue cheese crumbles on top of each serving for extra tang! This recipe is easily doubled to serve eight.

1-1/2 c. tomato juice, divided
3-oz. pkg. lemon gelatin mix
1/2 c. mild salsa

shredded lettuce
1/2 c. sour cream
2 T. cucumber, chopped

In a saucepan over medium heat, bring one cup tomato juice to a boil. Add gelatin mix, stirring to dissolve. Stir in remaining cold tomato juice and salsa; mix well. Pour into a deep 6"x6" plastic refrigerator container. Refrigerate until firm. Slice into 4 servings. Place on a bed of shredded lettuce. Combine sour cream and cucumber; spoon dressing over aspic. Serves 4.

As the summer sun sets, set out starry luminarias. Use a star-shaped punch to add holes to a paper lunch bag, then pour an inch of sand into the bottom. Tuck a tealight into a votive holder and light for a starry nighttime glow.

Best Friends' Greek Pasta

Rachel Hill
Center, TX

My best friend and I went to an Italian restaurant and ordered the Greek Pasta. We loved it so much that my friend went home and figured out how to make it. She passed this recipe on to me, and now every time I make it for socials everyone wants the recipe.

3 to 4 chicken breast fillets
Cajun seasoning to taste
16-oz. pkg. penne pasta, cooked
1/4 c. basil pesto sauce
2 T. garlic, minced

6-oz. jar pitted Kalamata olives, drained
8-oz. pkg. crumbled feta cheese
3/4 c. Italian salad dressing

Sprinkle chicken with seasoning. Grill until juices run clear; slice into bite-size pieces and set aside. While pasta is still hot, stir in pesto and garlic; mix well. Stir in remaining ingredients except salad dressing. Add dressing to coat; mix well. Serves 4 to 6.

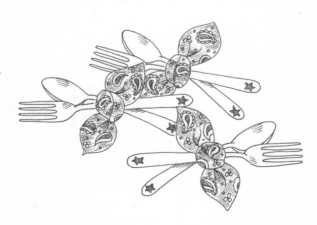

Bright bandannas make colorful summertime napkins...find them
in shades of blue, pink, yellow, red and green. Tie one around
each set of flatware for lap-size napkins, then, after lunch,
toss them in the washer...so easy!

Santa Fe Grilled Veggie Pizzas

*April Jacobs
Loveland, CO*

While waiting for a train in Santa Fe, we stopped for lunch at a little restaurant and ordered grilled vegetable pizza. It was so tasty, I had to find a way to recreate it when we returned home to our ranch in Colorado!

10-oz. tube refrigerated pizza
    crust
1 lb. portabella mushrooms,
    stems removed
1 red pepper, quartered
1 yellow pepper, quartered
1 zucchini, cut lengthwise into
    1/2-inch thick slices

1 yellow squash, cut lengthwise
    into 1/2-inch thick slices
3/4 t. salt
1 c. Alfredo sauce
1-1/4 c. smoked mozzarella
    cheese, shredded

Lightly dust 2 baking sheets with flour. On a lightly floured surface, press dough into a 15-inch by 11-inch rectangle. Cut into quarters; place 2 on each baking sheet. Lightly coat vegetables with non-stick vegetable spray; sprinkle with salt. Grill vegetables over medium-hot coals until tender, about 10 minutes. Cut mushrooms and peppers into slices. Cut squash in half crosswise. Grill 2 pieces pizza dough at a time for one minute, or until golden. With tongs, turn dough over and grill 30 seconds, or until firm. Return to baking sheets. Spread crusts with sauce; top with vegetables and cheese. Grill pizzas, covered, for 2 to 3 minutes, until cheese melts. Makes 4 servings.

When grilling veggies, baste them with a simple marinade that's big on flavor. Whisk together 1/2 cup melted butter, 1/2 cup lemon juice and one tablespoon freshly chopped basil.

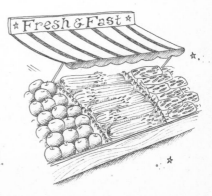

Golden Zucchini Patties

Edie DeSpain
Logan, UT

*Not the "usual" zucchini patties, these have such flavor
and bake up golden and delicious.*

3-1/2 c. zucchini, grated
3 T. onion, grated
2 T. fresh parsley, minced
1/3 c. grated Parmesan cheese
1 c. soft bread crumbs

1 t. salt
1/2 t. pepper
2 eggs, beaten
3/4 c. dry bread crumbs
1/2 c. butter, melted

Wrap zucchini in paper towels; press out as much liquid as possible.
Combine zucchini, onion, parsley, cheese, soft bread crumbs, salt,
pepper and eggs. Shape into patties; dip into dry bread crumbs. Place
on greased baking sheets; drizzle with butter. Bake at 350 degrees for
30 to 40 minutes, until golden. Makes 6 to 8.

Brand new terra cotta pots make super summer serving dishes.
Line with a tea towel, napkin or bandanna and fill with
fresh veggies, rolls, bread sticks, straws or silverware.

Fresh...From
THE GARDEN

Kit's Herbed Bread

Nola Coons
Gooseberry Patch

An herbed butter is a great way to dress up grilled corn on the cob, fresh veggies and warm rolls. My friend, Kit, makes this all the time.

6 T. butter, softened
2 T. fresh parsley, minced
2 green onions, finely chopped
2 t. fresh basil, minced

1 clove garlic, minced
1/4 t. pepper
1 loaf French bread, halved
    lengthwise

Combine all ingredients except bread in a small bowl; mix well. Spread on cut sides of bread. Place bread on an ungreased baking sheet. Broil 4 inches from heat for 2 to 3 minutes, or until golden. Keep refrigerated for up to 2 weeks, or will stay fresh in the freezer for one month. Makes 8 servings.

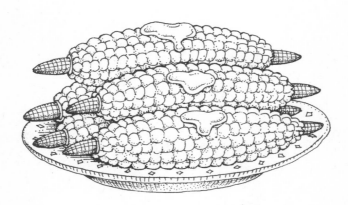

Corn on the cob...perfect every time! Bring a stockpot of water to a boil and add corn. When the water returns to a boil, remove the stockpot from heat, cover and set the timer for 5 minutes.

Homemade Tomato Soup

Helen Braley
Plymouth, ME

*My dear son loved my homemade soup. So much so, that he
wrote a story about it in high school and got an A.
He is very much missed by his family.*

1 peck or 15 lbs. ripe tomatoes
4 onions, chopped
6 to 8 whole cloves
4 t. celery salt
3 bay leaves
1 c. margarine

1-1/4 c. all-purpose flour
1 c. sugar
7 t. salt
1 t. pepper
12 1-pint canning jars and lids,
    sterilized

Combine first 5 ingredients in a large soup kettle; bring to a boil over
medium heat. Reduce heat; simmer for one hour. Remove from heat;
run mixture through a food mill. Process until smooth. Pour mixture
back into kettle; add margarine, stir until melted. Remove 4 cups
mixture to blender; add remaining ingredients. Blend until smooth;
pour back into kettle. Cook over medium heat, stirring often, for
about 5 minutes. Spoon soup into hot sterilized jars, leaving 1/4-inch
headspace. Wipe rims; secure with lids and rings. Process in a boiling
water bath for 15 minutes; set jars on a towel to cool. Check for seals.
Makes 12 jars.

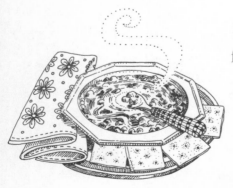

Keep all those garden fresh veggies
fresh longer. Most veggies should be
kept in the refrigerator with the
exception of potatoes, sweet
potatoes, onions and eggplant.
Tomatoes will also keep their
sun-ripened flavor best if stored
on the counter, not in the refrigerator.

Summer in a Bowl

Angie Cornelius
Sheridan, IL

We have a large, wonderful vegetable garden every summer, and I enjoy planting a section devoted to fresh herbs. This salad makes excellent use of all those peppers, cucumbers and tomatoes, plus lots of fresh basil. For us, it's truly "summer in a bowl!"

4 ripe roma tomatoes, seeded
   and chopped
1 cubanelle pepper, chopped
1 cucumber, chopped
1/4 c. red onion, minced

6 fresh basil leaves, shredded
salt and pepper to taste
4 c. French or Italian bread,
   toasted and cubed
3 T. olive oil

Combine vegetables, basil, salt and pepper to taste. Let stand at room temperature for 30 minutes. Stir in bread cubes; drizzle with oil. Mix thoroughly; serve at room temperature. Serves 4.

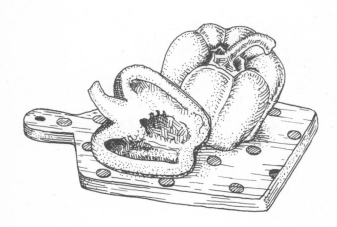

Serve individual servings of salads in hollowed-out bell peppers...
choose a variety of red, green, yellow and orange.

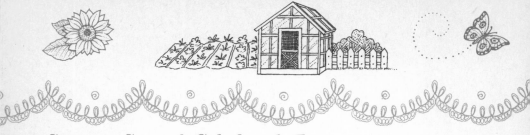

Summer Spinach Salad with Feta

Michelle Matuizek
Springdale, PA

When friends are coming over for lunch or dinner,
"wow" them with this summer salad!

9-oz. pkg. baby spinach
1-qt. container strawberries,
   hulled and sliced
2 c. blackberries
10-oz. pkg. chopped walnuts

2 8-oz. pkgs. crumbled feta
   cheese
16-oz. bottle raspberry-walnut
   vinaigrette
Garnish: 6-oz. pkg. croutons

Combine first 5 ingredients in a large salad bowl; gently toss. Add dressing to taste; sprinkle with croutons. Makes 7 servings.

Fruit and salads are terrific together. For a fast-fix fruit dip,
blend 8 ounces of softened cream cheese with a
7-1/2 ounce jar of marshmallow creme.

Penne-Pepper Pasta

Cheri Maxwell
Gulf Breeze, FL

If you like pasta with a little smoky flavor, char the pepper over a flame. Place it in a plastic zipping bag, then set aside for about 10 minutes...this makes it so easy to peel and seed.

2-1/2 c. penne pasta, cooked
1 c. roasted red pepper, cut into
    strips

1/2 c. pitted Kalamata olives

Prepare pasta according to package directions; drain. Toss pasta with pepper, olives, and sauce to taste. Serve hot or cold. Makes 6 servings.

Yogurt-Herb Sauce;

1 c. baby spinach
1/2 c. plain yogurt
1/2 c. crumbled feta
1/2 c. fresh parsley
3 T. fresh oregano

2 T. fresh mint
2 T. lemon juice
1 t. honey
salt and pepper to taste
1/4 c. olive oil

Combine all ingredients except oil in a food processor; process until finely chopped. Add oil; process until smooth.

If friends are visiting and your flower garden hasn't popped into bloom just yet, pick up flowers from the farmers' market. Tucked into jelly jars, shortly snipped blossoms look oh-so sweet.

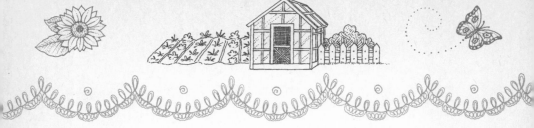

Amish Wedding Celery

Kathy Majeske
Denver, PA

An Amish friend of mine gave me this recipe a few years ago...it's a staple at Amish weddings, which are held in November. One can often tell if someone from the family will be getting married by looking at their gardens in the summer. If they're growing lots of celery, chances are there is an upcoming wedding!

8 c. celery, chopped
1 t. salt
1 c. water
1/2 c. sugar
2 t. vinegar

2 T. butter
1/2 c. evaporated milk
2-1/2 T. brown sugar, packed
2 T. all-purpose flour

Combine celery, salt, water, sugar and butter in a large saucepan over medium-high heat; bring to a boil. Reduce heat; simmer until celery is tender. Stir in remaining ingredients; cook until heated through. Serve warm. Makes 6 servings.

Slip seed packets and favorite garden photos among a length
of wire garden edging...so pretty over a mantel.

FOOD,
Family &
Friends

County Fair Maidrites

Samantha Moyer
Farragut, IA

*For many years my mom ran the 4-H food stand at our county fair.
We waited all year long for Mom to start cooking these. Even without
the fair, these are great for a crowd and they freeze well too.*

5 lbs. ground beef
1/2 c. onion, diced
2 T. salt
2 t. pepper
5 c. catsup
1/3 c. mustard

1/4 c. quick-cooking oats,
   uncooked
3 T. brown sugar, packed
2-1/2 t. Worcestershire sauce
20 to 25 hamburger buns, split

Brown ground beef in a large skillet over medium heat; drain. Add
onion, salt and pepper; cook until onion is transparent. Add remaining
ingredients except buns; stir and simmer until heated through. Spoon
onto buns. Makes 20 to 25 servings.

Family reunions are a summertime favorite...good food, family,
laughter and memories in the making. Set the date early,
at least 2 to 3 months in advance. This allows everyone
plenty of time to plan for vacations, school, weddings
and any other activities that are planned.

Food, Family
& FRIENDS

Beefy Cheddar Bake

Kimberly Keafer
Johnsbury, VT

This was my grandmother's casserole recipe. Mom made it for her family and now I make it for mine. It's delicious and a great dish for sharing. Everyone I've ever made this for loves it and asks to have it again. Go ahead, reheat it the next day, it's just as good!

1 lb. ground beef
1 onion, chopped
1 green pepper, chopped
14-1/2 oz. can diced tomatoes,
   drained
8-oz. pkg. shredded sharp
   Cheddar cheese

2 c. rotini pasta, cooked
10-3/4 oz. can cream of
   mushroom soup
6-oz. can French fried onions

In a skillet over medium-high heat, brown beef with onion and pepper; drain. Combine all ingredients except French fried onions in a large bowl; mix well. Spread mixture into a lightly greased 13"x9" baking pan; cover with aluminum foil. Bake at 350 degrees for 30 minutes. Remove foil; sprinkle with onions. Bake, uncovered, for an additional 5 to 10 minutes. Serves 8 to 12.

Make reunion invitations fun to open...tuck in favorite family photos, school pictures or wedding pictures. Be sure to include all the specifics...date, where, when and the time. And be sure to list anything that's needed...a favorite potluck dish, games, chairs or blankets.

Summer Tortellini Salad

Jen Eveland-Kupp
Blandon, PA

*Include any favorite veggies...a garnish of tomato wedges
or orange slices and parsley sprigs is nice.*

8-oz. pkg. cheese tortellini,
   cooked and cooled
1 tomato, chopped
3 to 4 slices hard salami, thinly
   sliced lengthwise
3 to 4 mushrooms, sliced
4 to 5 Kalamata olives, pitted
   and chopped
1/2-inch thick slice mild Cheddar cheese, cut into 1/2-inch
   cubes
1/2-inch thick slice of
   mozzarella cheese, cut into
   1/2-inch cubes

1/2-inch thick slice Provolone
   cheese, cut into 1/2-inch
   cubes
1/4 c. olive oil
1 clove garlic, finely minced
1/4 t. garlic salt
1/8 t. pepper
2 to 3 T. cider vinegar
Optional: 1 t. red pepper flakes

In a large bowl, combine tortellini, tomato, salami, mushrooms, olives
and cheeses; set aside. Whisk together oil, garlic, garlic salt, pepper,
vinegar and red pepper flakes, if using, until throughly mixed. Pour
over the salad; mix well. Refrigerate for a few hours to blend flavors.
Mix well again before serving. Makes 4 to 6 servings.

Top picnic tables with bouquets of cheery sunflowers, zinnias and
cosmos. The key to keeping them looking their best...an aspirin,
shiny penny or a drop of bleach in plain, room-temperature water.

4th of July Beans

Laurie Lightfoot
Hawthorne, NV

It's just not summer without this favorite side dish!

1 lb. bacon, diced
1 lb. ground beef
1 lb. hot ground pork sausage
1 c. onion, chopped
28-oz. can pork & beans
15-oz. can ranch-style beans
15-oz. can maple-flavored
   baked beans
16-oz. can kidney beans,
   drained and rinsed

1/2 c. barbecue sauce
1/2 c. catsup
1/2 c. brown sugar, packed
1 T. mustard
2 T. molasses
1 t. salt
1/2 t. chili powder

In a large skillet over medium heat, cook bacon, beef, sausage and onion until meat is browned; drain. Transfer to a greased disposable aluminum roasting pan. Stir in beans; mix well. In a small bowl, combine remaining ingredients; stir into bean mixture. Cover and bake at 350 degrees for 45 minutes. Uncover and bake for an additional 15 minutes. Makes 10 to 12 servings.

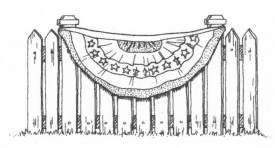

Reunions can be held just about anywhere...a park, backyard, barn or at the lake. Have plenty of tables and chairs on hand, hang the "Welcome!" sign, then get to the fun of decorating! Hang colorful banners and buntings, or drape cotton fabric from the trees for a simple awning.

Chow Mein Noodle Casserole

Vicki Cox
Bland, MO

*Passed down from my aunt, this recipe is always a favorite
at potlucks with no leftovers!*

2 lbs. ground beef
1 onion, chopped
10-3/4 oz. can cream of celery
   soup
10-3/4 oz. can golden
   mushroom soup

1-1/4 c. water
1/2 t. salt
1 c. instant rice, uncooked
1 T. Worcestershire sauce
1 t. garlic powder
5-oz. can chow mein noodles

Brown ground beef and onion in a large skillet over medium heat;
drain. Stir together remaining ingredients except chow mein noodles
in a large bowl. Add beef mixture; mix well. Transfer to a lightly
greased 13"x9" baking pan. Bake, uncovered, at 375 degrees for
20 minutes, until bubbly. Sprinkle with chow mein noodles; bake,
uncovered, for an additional 5 to 10 minutes. Makes 16 servings.

This super-simple table runner adds a cheerful look to tables.
Simply line up enough bandannas to fit the length
of a table, then stitch together. It's so simple and colorful!

Food, Family
& FRIENDS

Elaine's Oriental Noodle Salad

Elaine Slabinski
Monroe Township, NJ

This is a great summertime recipe and is a nice twist on the usual salads with mayonnaise in them. It may seem like a large salad, but it disappears fast!

1 head bok choy, chopped
4 green onions, sliced
1/4 c. butter
2 3-oz. pkgs. ramen noodles,
    uncooked and broken
1/2 t. sesame seed

8-oz. pkg. slivered almonds
1 c. oil
1 c. sugar
1/4 c. rice wine vinegar
2 t. soy sauce

Combine bok choy and onions in a large bowl; set aside. Melt butter in a large skillet over medium heat; add noodles, sesame seed and almonds. Sauté until golden; remove to a paper towel. Mix together ramen seasoning packets and remaining ingredients. Add noodle mixture to bok choy mixture; mix well. Whisk together oil, sugar, vinegar and soy sauce until sugar has dissolved. Drizzle over salad; gently toss to coat. Serves 12 to 15.

Summer breeze so softly blowing
In my garden pinks are growing,
If you'll go and send the showers,
You may come and smell my flowers.
    -Vintage Children's Book

Broccoli-Cranberry Salad

Dueley Lucas
Somerset, KY

This is the most-requested recipe at our family reunion and church socials. From the first time I made this salad, my friends and family have loved it and request it all the time.

3 bunches broccoli, chopped
1/2 c. sweetened dried
    cranberries
1/2 c. golden raisins
1/2 c. chopped walnuts
Optional: 1/2 c. sunflower seeds

Optional: 1 red onion, chopped
3/4 c. mayonnaise
1 T. cider vinegar
3 T. sugar
milk to taste

Combine broccoli, cranberries, raisins and walnuts. Add sunflower seeds and onion, if using; set aside. Mix together remaining ingredients in a blender adding enough milk until dressing is desired consistency. Process until well combined. Pour over broccoli mixture; gently toss to coat. Makes 4 servings.

When it's just too hot to cook, invite friends & neighbors over
for a salad potluck. Everyone brings along their favorite
salad to share, and you set up a table in a shady
spot and serve up frosty pink lemonade!

Southern Mexi-Salad

Cam Scott
Aurora, IN

My favorite to take to family reunions.

2 15-1/4 oz. cans corn, drained
2 16-oz. cans black beans,
    drained and rinsed
10-oz. can diced tomatoes with
    chiles
3/4 c. green onions, thinly sliced

1/3 c. olive oil
1/3 c. lime juice
1 T. fresh cilantro, minced
1 t. salt
1 t. ground cumin

Combine all ingredients in a large bowl; refrigerate until ready to serve. Serves 8 to 10.

Make a family tree...it's so easy. Slip a branch into a sap bucket filled with florists' foam, then hide the foam with pebbles. Dress up mailing tags with copies of family photos and newspaper clippings. Rubber stamp on names and dates, then tie onto the branches.

Pepper Jack Salsa

Kristi Townes
Union City, TN

I have been serving this salsa at gatherings of all kinds and everyone always asks for the recipe. It goes great at family dinners and get-togethers. The recipe makes a lot so it's great for a crowd, and when it's time to leave, the bowl is always empty.

14-1/2 oz. can petite diced
  tomatoes
2 10-oz. cans diced tomatoes
  with lime juice and cilantro
3.8-oz. can black olives sliced
  and coarsely chopped
2 8-oz. pkgs. shredded Pepper
  Jack cheese

16-oz. bottle zesty Italian salad
  dressing
Optional: 1/2 c. green onions,
  chopped
tortilla chips

Combine all ingredients except tortilla chips in a large bowl; mix well. Refrigerate until ready to serve. Serve with tortilla chips. Makes about 8 cups.

Have some activities planned for family reunions...softball games, touch football, 3-legged races or an egg & spoon race are great fun. Don't forget to bring along some board games, a deck of cards, checkers and scrapbooks for sharing too.

Purlieu

Cheri Mason
Harmony, NC

Pronounced Purr-Low, and also called Chicken Bog, this is a South Carolina Low Country recipe. Always a favorite dish found at church socials, family reunions, potlucks and family dinners.

14-oz. pkg. smoked sausage, sliced 1/4-inch thick
4 slices bacon, chopped
1 onion, chopped
4 c. chicken broth
4 boneless, skinless chicken breasts, cut into bite-size pieces

5-oz. pkg. saffron yellow rice, uncooked
1-1/4 c. long-cooking rice, uncooked

Combine sausage, bacon and onion in a large pot over medium heat. Sauté until onion is translucent. Add broth; bring to a boil. Stir in chicken; return to a boil again. Add rice; boil for one minute. Reduce heat to low; cover and cook for 20 minutes. Remove from heat; let stand covered for 10 minutes. Serves 8.

Let the fun begin! Bring along some crafts for the kids...and adults! Baskets of beads, construction paper, craft scissors, glue sticks, rubber stamps, pipe cleaners, die cuts, buttons and fabric scraps. It's fun to see all the clever creations that are made!

Chrissy's Ravishing Rhubarb Slush

Jen Sell
Farmington, MN

*This slush is so yummy! The recipe was given to me this summer
by a good friend, Chrissy...she and I love to exchange recipes,
and this one is easy to whip up when rhubarb is plentiful.*

8 c. rhubarb, sliced
2 qts. water
6-oz. pkg. strawberry gelatin
   mix

1/2 c. lemon juice
3 c. sugar
2 2-ltr. bottles lemon-lime soda,
   chilled

Combine rhubarb and water in a large pot; bring to a boil. Cook for
15 to 20 minutes. Strain, reserving juice. Add gelatin mix to juice; stir
in lemon juice and sugar. Pour into an ice cream pail. Freeze, stirring
every couple hours until set. Spoon slush into glasses, filling half full;
pour soda over top, filling glass. Makes 25 to 30 servings.

If it looks like it's going to be hot weather, whip up a basket full
of hand fans for everyone to pick and choose from. Wallpaper
scraps, fabric snippets and copies of handwritten recipes are
perfect for arranging on posterboard. Use a spray adhesive
to secure them, then glue on a paint stir-stick handle.

Citrus Tea Punch

Ellie Brandel
Milwaukie, OR

I like to serve this at our summer get-togethers...
a nice change from regular ice tea.

2 qts. water
16 teabags
12-oz. can frozen lemonade
   concentrate
12-oz. can frozen limeade
   concentrate

2 c. cranberry juice cocktail,
   chilled
2 2-ltr. bottles ginger ale, chilled
ice ring

Bring water to a boil over high heat; pour over teabags that have been placed in a large bowl. Steep for 5 minutes; remove and discard teabags. Refrigerate tea until well chilled. Pour iced tea into a punch bowl. Stir in concentrates until dissolved. Add cranberry juice. Just before serving, add ginger ale and ice ring. Makes 20 to 25 servings.

If you plan to display a flag at a 4th of July family reunion, remember the banner of stars should be positioned in top upper left-hand corner when you face the flag.

Friendship Casserole

*April King
Eugene, OR*

*Passed from friend-to-friend through the years, this recipe has been
shared at every get-together from potlucks to church suppers.*

1/2 c. butter	7-oz. can chopped green chiles
10 eggs	16-oz. container cottage cheese
1/2 c. all-purpose flour	2 8-oz. pkgs. shredded
1 t. baking powder	Monterey Jack cheese
1/8 t. salt	

Melt butter in a 13"x9" baking pan, spreading evenly. Beat eggs in a
large bowl; stir in flour, baking powder and salt until well blended.
Add melted butter and remaining ingredients; mix just until blended.
Pour into pan and bake, uncovered, at 400 degrees for 15 minutes;
reduce temperature to 350 degrees. Bake for an additional 35 to
40 minutes. Cut into squares and serve hot. Serves 10 to 12.

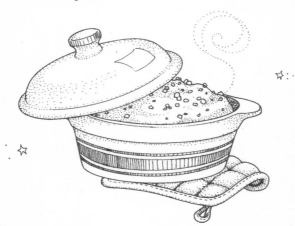

Ask everyone to jot down favorite stories and slip them into a
memory envelope decorated with vintage-style papers, rubber
stamps, rick rack, buttons and ribbon. Pulled out and read
one at a time, they'll bring lots of sweet remembrances.

Texas Corn & Green Chile Casserole

Terri King
Granger, TX

Always requested at every church potluck...this casserole is so easy and extremely tasty. It's a must at our summer family barbecues.

8-oz. pkg. cream cheese
1/4 c. butter
1/4 c. sugar

16-oz. pkg. frozen corn, thawed
7-oz. can diced green chiles
salt and pepper to taste

Combine cream cheese, butter and sugar in a medium saucepan over medium heat; cook until melted. Add corn and chiles; stir until well blended. Sprinkle with salt and pepper. Pour into a greased 1-1/2 quart casserole dish. Bake, uncovered, at 350 degrees for 30 to 40 minutes, until golden around edges. Serves 10.

Serve up frosty lemonade or herbal ice tea with blueberry skewers.
Simply slide blueberries onto a wooden skewer until covered;
top with a fresh mint leaf...easy!

Mom's Sandwich Spread

Karen Vasicak
Swoyersville, PA

My mother often made these sandwiches for us as kids...they're great to take on trips and enjoy with a bag of potato chips. There are a lot of sandwich spread recipes; however, Mom's recipe is different because it includes a green pepper...it adds a tasty spin to the usual sandwich spread flavor.

1 lb. bologna, coarsely chopped
1 onion, coarsely chopped
16-oz. jar sweet pickles, drained
   and coarsely chopped
1 green pepper, coarsely
   chopped

mayonnaise-style salad dressing
   to taste
1 loaf sliced white bread

Combine all ingredients except salad dressing and bread in a meat grinder. Process to desired consistency. Stir in salad dressing to taste. Assemble sandwiches. Makes 8 to 12.

Make sandwiches ahead of time, slip them into wax paper bags
and tuck into a vintage picnic tin...easy to tote and ready
to enjoy when you arrive at the reunion!

Church Ladies' Ham Salad

Ruby Shepley
Shamokin, PA

The women of St. James have been making this recipe
ever since I can remember.

6 lbs. bologna, chopped
1 stalk celery, finely chopped
1 doz. eggs, hard-boiled, peeled
    and diced
pickle relish to taste
32-oz. jar sweet pickles, drained
    and chopped

3 onions, minced
32-oz. jar mayonnaise-style
    salad dressing
9 to 10 loaves sliced white,
    wheat or sourdough bread

Place bologna in a food processor; process until well ground. Combine
ground bologna with remaining ingredients except bread; mix well.
Spread on half the bread slices; top with remaining bread slices.
Makes 7 to 8 dozen.

Bring along a variety of breads so everyone can choose their
favorite for spreading with ham salad and sandwich spreads. Sliced
bagels, Hawaiian sweet bread, party rye, pita pockets, wraps and
hearty country white bread all make delicious sandwiches.

Mom's Baked Beans

Dawn Spitler
South Point, OH

Every summer at family reunions, these baked beans are what Mom was always asked to bring. As a matter of fact, they even became a part of our very large family Thanksgiving meals! I try to keep the tradition by preparing this recipe every summer, and I have even taught my 14-year-old daughter how to make them so she can continue the tradition.

4 to 6 slices bacon, chopped
1 onion, chopped
1 lb. ground beef chuck
5 14-1/2 oz. cans pork & beans

1 c. dark corn syrup
1/2 c. catsup
2 t. mustard
1/8 t. Worcestershire sauce

Brown bacon, onion and ground beef in a large skillet over medium heat; drain and set aside. In a large bowl, mix together remaining ingredients; stir in ground beef mixture. Spread into a greased 13"x9" baking pan. Bake, uncovered, at 350 degrees for 45 minutes, until hot and bubbly. Makes 12 to 15 servings.

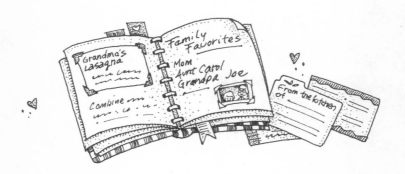

Jot down favorite recipes, ones that have been handed down, and make copies to share when family & friends are together. Invite others to bring their recipes to share too...it's a great way to preserve those that are time-tested and bring back the sweetest memories.

Tonya's Must-Have Potato-Corn Bake

Tonya Lewis
Scottsburg, IN

When we have big gatherings with my family, we all have special foods that we are expected to bring...this is mine and 99% of the time, the dish goes home empty!

1/2 lb. bacon, coarsely chopped
1/2 c. green pepper, finely
   chopped
1/3 c. onion, finely chopped
15-oz. can creamed corn
2 c. milk
3 T. butter

3/4 t. salt
1/8 t. pepper
2 c. instant mashed potato
   flakes
1/2 c. sour cream
1/4 c. grated Parmesan cheese
2 T. green onion, finely chopped

Cook bacon in a large skillet over medium heat until crisp. Remove bacon from pan, reserving one tablespoon drippings. Add green pepper and onion to drippings; cook over medium heat until tender. Stir in corn, milk, butter, salt and pepper; cook over medium heat until mixture is hot and bubbly. Remove from heat; stir in potato flakes and sour cream until well blended. Spoon mixture into a greased 11"x7" baking pan; top with bacon, Parmesan cheese and green onion. Bake, covered, at 375 degrees for 20 to 25 minutes, or until heated through. Serves 6.

A trio of flickering votives that look like fireflies! Slip votives into Mason jars, then thread wire around the jar rims to create a loop for hanging. Oh-so pretty on a summer's evening.

Midwestern Zucchini Casserole

Jackie Selover
Sidney, OH

This is a recipe I use when zucchini is abundant in the summer and my family loves it. Very versatile, try mushrooms or garlic... really any kind of vegetable you have in your garden.

1 onion, chopped
1 green or red pepper, chopped
3 c. zucchini, cubed
2 T. oil
1 lb. ground beef

2 8-oz. cans tomato sauce
2 c. brown rice, uncooked
salt and pepper to taste
Garnish: grated Parmesan
  cheese

In a skillet over medium heat, sauté onion, pepper and zucchini in oil; remove from pan. Add beef to skillet; cook until no longer pink. Drain. Combine vegetable mixture, beef and remaining ingredients except cheese in a slow cooker. Cover and cook on low setting for 3 hours. Garnish with cheese before serving. Serves 6.

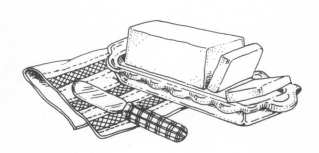

When serving rolls alongside main dishes, dress up 1/2 cup of butter by softening it, then blending in 2 teaspoons orange or tangerine zest. Place butter on a sheet of wax paper and roll into a log shape. Chill for 2 to 3 hours until firm. Store any leftovers in the refrigerator for up to 2 days.

Oh-So-Hot Banana Peppers

Jean Cerutti
Kittanning, PA

My friend, Sherry, brought this to our summer pool party and it has been my family's favorite ever since. For a milder version, use mild banana peppers and sweet sausage...it's still wonderful!

18 hot banana peppers
2 6-oz. pkgs. pork-flavored stuffing mix, prepared
2 lbs. ground hot pork sausage, browned and drained
1 onion, chopped

1 zucchini, chopped
2 eggs, beaten
1/2 c. brown sugar, packed
16-oz. pkg. shredded Cheddar cheese

Slice peppers down center of one side lengthwise to open up; run under water, removing seeds. Combine prepared stuffing and sausage in a large bowl; add onion and zucchini. Stir in eggs and brown sugar; mix well. Spoon into peppers; arrange peppers in a lightly greased 13"x9" baking pan. Bake, uncovered, at 350 degrees for 1-1/2 hours. Sprinkle with cheese; bake for an additional 10 minutes, or until cheese is melted. Makes 12 servings.

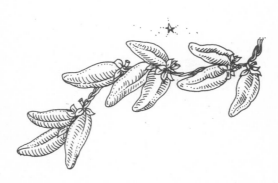

When making any dish with hot peppers as an ingredient, it's always a good idea to wear a pair of plastic gloves to protect your skin while cutting, slicing or chopping the peppers. Just toss away the gloves when preparation is all done.

Boycott-Your-Grill Beef Kabobs

Kathy Solka
Ishpeming, MI

Skewers that bake in the oven...perfect for a rained-out cookout!

1 c. oil
2/3 c. soy sauce
1/2 c. lemon juice
1/4 c. Worcestershire sauce
1/4 c. mustard
2 cloves garlic, minced
1 T. pepper
1/8 t. hot pepper sauce

3 lbs. beef sirloin steak, cut into
   2-inch cubes
2 green peppers, cut into 1-inch
   squares
2 8-oz. pkgs. mushrooms
20-oz. can pineapple chunks,
   drained

Combine all ingredients except steak, vegetables and pineapple. Pour over steak; cover and refrigerate for 24 hours. Thread steak, vegetables and pineapple onto skewers. Arrange on greased baking sheets. Bake at 400 degrees for 8 to 10 minutes. Turn and continue baking until steak is done. Makes 4 servings.

There's always such great food at family reunions that we all
want to try a bit of everything! To help out, try making
bite-size burgers, two-bite brownies and cut wooden
skewers in half for mini kabobs...perfect!

Food, Family
& FRIENDS

BLT Macaroni Salad

Tina Sarama
Sloan, NY

Such a wonderful salad that I double the recipe for summer parties!

16-oz. pkg. macaroni, cooked
1-1/4 c. celery, diced
5 green onions, finely chopped
1 tomato, diced
1-1/4 c. mayonnaise

5 t. white vinegar
1/4 t. salt
1/8 t. pepper
Garnish: 1 lb. bacon, crisply
   cooked and crumbled

In a large bowl, combine macaroni, celery, onions and tomato. In a separate bowl, combine remaining ingredients except bacon; pour over macaroni mixture, tossing to coat. Cover and chill for at least 2 hours. Just before serving, sprinkle with bacon. Serves 6 to 8.

For just-right individual servings, spoon veggie or
fruit salads into one-pint Mason jars.

Ravioli Taco Bake

Margie Kirkman
High Point, NC

I was looking for something easy and different to take to our church potluck supper so I came up with this recipe. Not only was it a hit...I came home with an empty dish and over 50 people wanting the recipe!

1-1/2 lbs. ground beef	40-oz. can meat-filled ravioli
1-1/4 oz. pkg. taco seasoning mix	8-oz. pkg. shredded Cheddar cheese
3/4 c. water	Optional: sliced black olives

Brown ground beef in a large skillet over medium heat; drain. Stir in seasoning mix and water. Reduce heat; simmer for 8 to 10 minutes. Place ravioli in a lightly greased 13"x9" baking pan; spoon beef mixture over top. Sprinkle with cheese. Bake, uncovered, at 350 degrees for 25 to 30 minutes, until cheese is melted and bubbly. If desired, sprinkle with olives before serving. Serves 6 to 8.

Fun polka-dotty paper napkins and matching plates make for a table set with whimsy...and make clean-up a breeze!

Super-Simple Baked Peppers

Crystal Branstrom
Russell, PA

This is one of my favorite recipes to make during the summer when green peppers are fresh and plentiful.

3 green peppers, quartered
1 lb. ground beef
1/2 lb. ground Italian pork
   sausage
2 onions, chopped
garlic powder to taste

salt and pepper to taste
26-oz. jar spaghetti sauce
2 c. long-cooking rice, cooked
16-oz. pkg. pasteurized process
   cheese spread, sliced

Arrange peppers in a lightly greased 13"x9" baking pan; set aside. In a large skillet over medium heat, brown ground beef, sausage and onions with garlic powder, salt and pepper; drain. Stir in sauce and rice. Pour over peppers; top with sliced cheese. Cover with aluminum foil. Bake at 350 degrees for one hour. Serves 6 to 8.

A treat that's perfect for get-togethers. Spread 2 tablespoons of peanut butter on a tortilla, top with 1/4 cup of mini marshmallows and 2 tablespoons of chocolate chips. Roll up, wrap in aluminum foil and seal tightly. Bake at 375 degrees for 5 to 10 minutes, or until chocolate chips and marshmallows are melted. Yum!

Mandy's Easy Cheesy Chicken Casserole
Mandy Wheeler
Ashland, KY

This is a recipe that I created by combining a few different recipes.
My husband loves it and it is always a hit at reunions and potlucks.

3 to 4 cooked chicken breasts,
  chopped
16-oz. pkg. wide egg noodles,
  cooked
2 10-3/4 oz. cans cream of
  chicken soup
24-oz. container sour cream
8-oz. pkg. shredded Cheddar
  cheese

8-oz. pkg. shredded mozzarella
  cheese
1 sleeve round buttery crackers,
  crushed
1/4 c. margarine, melted
2 T. poppy seed

Combine chicken, noodles, soup, sour cream and cheeses in a large
bowl. Pour into a lightly greased 13"x9" baking pan. Mix together
cracker crumbs and margarine; sprinkle over top. Sprinkle poppy seed
over cracker crumbs. Bake at 350 degrees for 25 to 30 minutes, until
crackers are crispy and golden and cheese is melted. Serves 6 to 8.

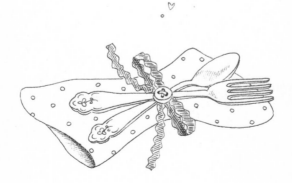

Dress up even paper napkins in a snap...just tie on a tiny bundle
of fragrant herbs. Even paper cups can be dressed up for
the occasion with a wrap of ribbon and a button.

Prize-Winning Pineapple Cheddar Bake

Marta May
Anderson, IN

This recipe has been in my family for a very long time, and I even won 2nd place when I entered it in a Dairy Council contest. My family always requests it when we have our May Family reunion. This year we are getting ready for the 120th consecutive reunion held in the original place in North Vernon, Indiana.

2 20-oz. cans pineapple tidbits
3/4 c. all-purpose flour
1 c. sugar
8-oz. pkg. shredded Cheddar
   cheese

3/4 c. margarine, melted
1 sleeve round buttery crackers,
   crushed

Spread pineapple into a greased 2-quart casserole. Mix together flour, sugar and cheese; add to pineapple, stirring well. Combine margarine and cracker crumbs; spread over pineapple mixture. Bake, covered, at 350 degrees for 30 minutes. Serve hot or cold. Makes 8 servings.

Be sure to bring along a camera and video camera to capture all the reunion fun and memories. Have disposable cameras on hand too so everyone, even little ones, can join in on the picture-taking fun. You'll be delighted at the terrific results!

Sicilian Salad

Denise Eagan
Huntington, WV

Every time I take this refreshing salad to our church or a family gathering, I have several requests for the recipe.

14-1/2 oz. can whole green
  beans, drained
1 to 2 15-oz. cans sliced
  potatoes, drained
1 to 2 red onions, chopped
4 tomatoes, cut into bite-size
  pieces

2 cucumbers, sliced
1/2 c. pitted Kalamata olives
1/2 t. Italian seasoning
1 to 2 c. red wine vinaigrette
  salad dressing

Layer vegetables in order listed in a large bowl; sprinkle with Italian seasoning. Pour salad dressing to taste over top; cover. Chill for several hours up to overnight. Before serving, toss to mix. Makes 6 to 8 servings.

Shake together the ingredients for this herbal vinaigrette in a Mason jar...done in a jiffy. Combine 1/3 cup olive oil, 1/4 cup white-wine vinegar, 2 teaspoons fresh thyme, basil or chives, one teaspoon Dijon mustard, one clove minced garlic, one teaspoon sugar and salt & pepper to taste; tighten lid and shake well.

Come By For **PIE**
...& More!

Lazy Daisy Cake

Jennifer Lemon
Lexington, OH

My grandma used to make this cake. She loved to cook and this recipe brings back all those memories of being in her kitchen.

1-1/4 c. boiling water
1 c. long-cooking oats, uncooked
1/2 c. margarine, softened
1 c. sugar
1 c. brown sugar, packed
1 t. vanilla extract

2 eggs, beaten
1-1/2 c. all-purpose flour
1 t. baking soda
1/2 t. salt
3/4 t. cinnamon
1/4 t. nutmeg

Pour water over oats; cover and let stand 20 minutes. Beat margarine until creamy; gradually add sugars and beat until fluffy. Blend in vanilla and eggs. Add oat mixture; mix well. Sift together flour, baking soda, salt, cinnamon and nutmeg; add to margarine mixture. Mix well. Pour batter into a well greased and floured 9"x9" baking pan. Bake at 350 degrees for 50 to 55 minutes, until a toothpick inserted near center comes out clean. Spread frosting on hot cake; broil until frosting is bubbly. Makes 8 to 10 servings.

Frosting:

1/4 c. margarine, melted
1/2 c. brown sugar, packed
3 T. half-and-half

1/3 c. chopped nuts
3/4 c. sweetened flaked coconut

Combine all ingredients; mix well.

To make sure that a frosted cake stays its prettiest, refrigerate it for one hour before slicing...it'll give the frosting time to firm up.

Bee Sting Cake   *Jo Ann*

This is a shorter version of an all-time favorite.

2 eggs, beaten
1 c. sugar
1 t. vanilla extract
1 c. all-purpose flour

1 t. baking powder
1/2 c. milk
2 T. butter

Beat together eggs, sugar, vanilla, flour and baking powder in a large bowl; set aside. Bring milk and butter to a boil in a saucepan over medium heat; mix well. Add to egg mixture; pour into a greased, floured 8"x 8" pan. Bake at 350 degrees for 30 minutes, or until a toothpick inserted near center tests done. Spread topping over warm cake. Broil until topping is bubbly and warm. Serves 10.

Topping:

1/2 c. plus 2 T. brown sugar,
  packed
1/4 c. butter, melted

1/4 c. whipping cream
1 c. sweetened flaked coconut
1 t. vanilla extract

Mix together all ingredients; mix well.

To keep cakes fresh for up to one week, they should be wrapped or covered and stored in the refrigerator. If stored on the counter under a cake dome or cake keeper, they'll stay fresh for about 3 days.

Soft & Chewy Pineapple Cookies

Carolyn Cochran
Dresden, OH

This is a recipe that was a big hit with my "Pop" when I was at home in the 1950's. It is easy and makes a soft chewy cookie that is sure to be a favorite with old and young alike.

1-1/2 c. sugar
1/2 c. shortening
1/2 c. crushed pineapple
2 eggs, beaten

1 t. baking powder
1/2 t. baking soda
1/2 t. salt
2 c. all-purpose flour

Mix all ingredients well. Drop dough the size of an egg on ungreased baking sheets. Bake at 350 degrees for 12 to 14 minutes, or until tops are lightly golden. Makes 3 to 4 dozen.

Super-simple ice cream sandwiches! Place a scoop of softened ice cream on the flat bottom of one side of a cookie. Top with another cookie, bottom-side down; press gently. Serve immediately or wrap and freeze for up to one week.

Watermelon Slice Cookies

Kay Barg
Sandy, UT

Sure to be a hit at any summertime get-together.

3/4 c. butter, softened
3/4 c. sugar
1 egg
1/2 t. almond extract
2 c. all-purpose flour
1/4 t. baking powder

1/8 t. salt
red and green gel food coloring
1/3 c. mini semi-sweet chocolate
   chips
1 t. sesame seed

Blend butter and sugar in a large mixing bowl. Beat in egg and extract; set aside. Combine flour, baking powder and salt; gradually add to butter mixture. Set aside one cup dough. Tint remaining dough with red food coloring and shape into a 3-1/2 inch diameter log; wrap in plastic wrap. Tint 1/3 cup reserved dough with green food coloring; wrap in plastic wrap. Wrap remaining plain dough and refrigerate all 3 doughs for 2 hours, or until firm. On a lightly floured surface, roll plain dough into an 8-1/2 inch by 3-1/2 inch rectangle. Place red dough log on the end of one short side of rectangle: roll up. Roll green dough into a 10-inch by 3-1/2 inch rectangle. Place red and white log on the end of the short side on green dough; roll up. Wrap in plastic wrap; refrigerate overnight. Unwrap and cut into 3/16-inch thick slices. Place 2 inches apart on ungreased baking sheets. Place chocolate chips and sesame seed on red part of dough to resemble seeds. Bake at 350 degrees for 9 to 11 minutes, or until firm. Immediately slice cookies in half. Cool. Makes 3 dozen.

Bring your own ants to a family picnic! Kids big & little will be delighted when they find yummy cookies tucked inside a big bug bucket! Simply arrange bug stickers, or hot glue plastic bugs, on an empty plastic ice cream bucket with a lid.

Aunt Elaine's Pink Lemonade Pie

Kathy Sharp
Westerville, OH

The recipe for this delicious pie was handed down to us from my husband's great-aunt Elaine...we think of her every time we make it. So easy and so refreshing, our daughter even won an award at a dessert competition by making this wonderful concoction.

6-oz. can frozen pink lemonade
    concentrate, thawed
14-oz. can sweetened
    condensed milk
8-oz. container frozen whipped
    topping, thawed

1/4 t. red food coloring
Optional: 1/4 to 1 t. lemon
    extract
Garnish: red decorating sugar
9-inch graham cracker crust

Mix lemonade concentrate, condensed milk, whipped topping and food coloring together until well blended. If desired, stir in lemon extract to taste, for a more tart flavor. Pour into graham cracker crust; sprinkle with decorating sugar. Cover and freeze for 4 hours to overnight. Thaw slightly before serving to make slicing easier. Makes 8 to 12 servings.

To quickly prepare a homemade graham cracker crust, place
24 graham crackers in a plastic zipping bag and roll them with
a rolling pin. Add 1/4 cup sugar and 6 tablespoons melted butter.

Summertime Strawberry Pie

Christina Hubbell
Jackson, MI

This recipe is always a family favorite.

1 qt. strawberries, hulled and
    divided
1 c. sugar
3 T. cornstarch

3-oz. pkg. cream cheese,
    softened
9-inch pie crust, baked
Garnish: whipped cream

Reserve half of the biggest strawberries, set aside. Put remaining strawberries, about 1-1/2 cups, in a blender. Process until smooth. If needed, add water to puréed berries to equal 2 cups; pour into a small saucepan. Add sugar and cornstarch; bring to a boil, stirring, for one minute. Remove from heat; cool. Spread cream cheese in bottom of pie crust; arrange reserved berries on top, pointed-end up. Pour cooled strawberry sauce over top. Refrigerate for 2 hours. To serve, top with whipped cream. Serves 6 to 8.

While strawberries are plentiful, whip up a recipe for Flamingo Punch...it's so easy. In a blender, combine one cup hulled strawberries, one cup diced, seeded watermelon, 1/2 cup orange juice and 1 tablespoon lime juice; mix at medium-high speed until puréed; strain. Stir in one cup chilled club soda and serve.

Flowerpot Cupcakes

JoAnna Nicoline-Haughey
Berwyn, PA

My children love to share these with their classmates
for a special birthday treat.

18-1/2 oz. pkg. favorite-flavor
   cake mix
20 flat-bottomed ice cream
   cones
16-oz. container favorite-flavor
   frosting

20 lollipops, unwrapped
20 spearmint candy leaves

Prepare cake mix as directed on package. Fill ice cream cones 3/4 full.
Arrange on ungreased baking sheets. Bake at 350 degrees for 18 to
20 minutes. Cool and frost cupcakes. Insert a lollipop into the center
of each cupcake. Slice candy leaves in half; press one to each side of
the lollipop stick to look like a flower leaf. Makes 20.

For the sweetest cupcake toppers, simply cut paper daisies from
construction paper and slip a lollipop through the center of each.
"Plant" the flowers in the center of each cupcake...so creative!

Come By
FOR PIE ...& More!

Muddy Pies

Rhonda Millerman
Cameron, WI

When I was growing up with my three sisters and two brothers, Mom always took time to make these for us. After school we'd find them still cooling on the wax paper...sometimes I'd scoop them up with a spoon to eat while they were still warm. Yum! What a great memory.

1/2 c. milk
3 T. baking cocoa
2 c. sugar
1/2 c. creamy peanut butter

1/2 c. butter
2 c. long-cooking oats, uncooked
1 t. vanilla extract

Place milk, baking cocoa and sugar in a saucepan over medium heat; bring to a boil. Boil for 3 minutes. Remove from heat; add peanut butter, butter, oats and vanilla. Mix well. Cool until stiff enough to drop by spoonfuls onto wax paper. Cool. Makes about 2 dozen.

When making a favorite cookie recipe, shake it up a bit to create something new. If a recipe calls for peanuts, try chocolate-covered peanuts, or toss in mint chocolate or peanut butter chips instead of milk chocolate chips.

Coney Island Egg Cream

Arlene Smulski
Lyons, IL

This soda-fountain classic contains no egg or cream. The name refers to the foamy head that looks like an egg white.

2 T. chocolate syrup   1/3 c. seltzer water
1 c. milk

Pour syrup into a tall glass; stir in milk. Add seltzer water; use an iced tea spoon to stir quickly and thoroughly until foamy. Makes one serving.

Apple Cider Floats

Pat Martin
Riverside, CA

I created this recipe about 20 years ago to use up some extra vanilla ice cream. The family liked it so well, I have been serving it ever since. It tastes like apple pie à la mode. With only three ingredients, you can always have them on hand to serve to unexpected guests or for an evening treat.

25.4-oz. bottle sparkling apple   Garnish: cinnamon
    cider
1/2 gal. vanilla ice cream

For each serving, pour 1/4 cup cider into a tall glass or mug. Add 2 scoops ice cream; sprinkle with cinnamon. Slowly top ice cream with remaining cider (it will fizz up). Serve with a long spoon. Makes 6 servings.

Fruit cubes are delicious in lemonades and juice drinks.
Fill ice cube trays with favorite juice and freeze. Mix
& match flavors to create a brand new flavor!

Walnuts in Sugar Syrup

Vickie

A delicious ice cream topping originating in New York and New Jersey...scrumptious!

1 c. light corn syrup
1 c. brown sugar, packed
3 T. butter

1/2 c. milk
1 t. vanilla extract
2 c. chopped walnuts

In a heavy saucepan, bring corn syrup, brown sugar, butter and milk to a slow boil over medium heat, stirring well. Lightly boil for 5 minutes; remove from heat. Add vanilla and nuts, stir well and let cool. Keep refrigerated. Serves 16.

Set out a variety of ice cream toppings so everyone can choose their favorites...chopped nuts, shredded coconut, maraschino cherries, sliced bananas or strawberries and chocolate chips.

Frosted Mango-Banana Bars

Lane McLoud
Siloam Springs, AR

*I entered this tropical treat in a contest at the state fair
and won first place!*

1/2 c. butter, softened
1-1/2 c. sugar
2 eggs, room temperature
8-oz. container plain yogurt
1-1/2 t. vanilla extract
2 c. all-purpose flour
1 t. baking soda

1/4 t. salt
1 ripe mango, pitted, peeled and
   mashed
2 ripe bananas, mashed
1/2 c. sweetened flaked coconut
Garnish: toasted coconut

In a large bowl, blend margarine and sugar; add eggs, yogurt and vanilla. Sift together flour, baking soda and salt; gradually add to margarine mixture. Stir in mango, bananas and coconut. Spread into a 15"x10" jelly-roll pan that has been sprayed with non-stick vegetable spray. Bake at 350 degrees for 20 to 25 minutes, until a toothpick comes out clean. Cool completely. Spread frosting over top; sprinkle with toasted coconut, if desired. Store in refrigerator. Cut into bars to serve. Makes 3 dozen.

Frosting:

8-oz. pkg. cream cheese,
   softened
1/2 c. butter, softened

2 t. vanilla extract
1/2 c. sweetened flaked coconut
3-3/4 c. powdered sugar

Beat cream cheese, butter and vanilla together in a large bowl. Gradually beat in powdered sugar to a smooth consistency. Stir in coconut.

Plant thyme between the stones in your walkway for a
sweet fragrance you'll notice with each step you take.

Come By
FOR PIE ...& More!

Grandma Smith's Frostsicles

Lori Crawford
Sebring, FL

When I was young, my Mom made this recipe for us during the hot summer, but never often enough for me as a 6-year-old! The "red" flavors...strawberry, raspberry and cherry, were the best. I would sit in the shade on the steps of the front porch, trying hard not to share any drips with the ants. Now I make them for my children, but not often enough, I'm sure.

3-oz. pkg. favorite-flavor gelatin
   mix
.23-oz. pkg. unsweetened
   flavored drink mix

1/2 to 1 c. sugar
2 c. very hot water
2 c. cold water

In a bowl, mix together all ingredients except cold water until completely dissolved. Stir in cold water. Pour into cups or trays and freeze. If freezer pop molds are used, dip briefly into warm water for easier removal from molds. Makes 6 to 12.

Icy treats are always welcome during the long, hot days of summer. For picnic fun, tuck wrapped ice cream sandwiches and other frozen goodies into a pail filled with crushed ice to keep them frosty.

Butterscotch Picnic Cake

Cindy Neel
Gooseberry Patch

In memory of my grandmother, Blanche Crago, this recipe was one of her collection that she gathered from family & friends.

1/2 c. butter
1 c. brown sugar, packed
3 eggs, beaten
1 t. vanilla extract
2 c. all-purpose flour
1 t. baking soda

1 t. salt
1-1/2 c. buttermilk
1 c. quick-cooking oats, uncooked
6-oz. pkg. butterscotch chips
1/3 c. chopped walnuts

Beat together butter and brown sugar until light and fluffy. Blend in eggs and vanilla; mix well. Whisk together flour, baking soda and salt; add to butter mixture alternately with buttermilk mixing well after each addition. Stir in oats. Pour into a greased 13"x9" baking pan. Combine butterscotch chips and nuts; sprinkle over top. Bake at 350 degrees for 30 to 35 minutes. Cool before serving. Serves 15 to 18.

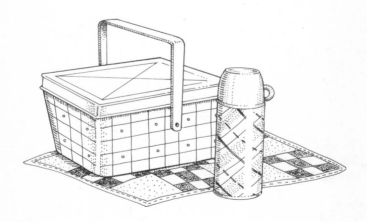

Vintage tin picnic baskets are terrific...so roomy, they easily tote goodies to & from a picnic, wipe clean in a jiffy and can be found in a variety of colors and fun patterns.

Cappuccino Mousse Pie

Jo Ann Tobias
Cogan Station, PA

This pie is so easy to make and enjoy on a hot summer day. A friend from work brought this one day to share and was kind enough to share the recipe too! You can really get creative by combining different flavors of pudding and coffee.

1/4 c. French vanilla coffee
   drink mix
2 c. milk, divided
2 3.4-oz. pkgs. instant French
   vanilla pudding mix

8-oz. container frozen whipped
   topping, thawed
9-inch graham cracker crust
Optional: chocolate curls

Blend together French vanilla coffee drink mix and 1/4 cup milk in a medium bowl; stir until well blended. Stir in pudding mix and remaining milk; whisk for 2 minutes. Add 3/4 cup whipped topping; spread into pie crust. Refrigerate for one hour, or until firm. Spread remaining whipped topping over pie. Garnish with chocolate curls, if desired. Store in refrigerator. Serves 8.

Treat yourself to root beer floats
this summer. Tall glasses
filled with scoops of vanilla ice
cream and chilled root beer
are a warm-weather must.
Shop at a nearby party
supply store to find some
whimsical straws!

Fresh Strawberry Shortcake

Nancy Ramsey
Gooseberry Patch

No doubt, one of the best things about summer hands down. Our strawberry patch has become so large, I've shared lots of plants, and this recipe, with all our friends & neighbors!

1 qt. strawberries, hulled and sliced
1 c. sugar, divided
2 c. all-purpose flour
4 t. baking powder
1/4 t. salt
1/8 t. nutmeg
1/2 c. butter
1/2 c. milk
2 eggs, separated
2 c. sweetened whipped cream
Optional: fresh mint sprigs

Gently stir together strawberries and 1/2 cup sugar; chill. Combine flour, 1/4 cup sugar, baking powder, salt and nutmeg; cut in butter until crumbly. Combine milk and egg yolks; mix well. Add to flour mixture, stirring just until moistened. Divide dough in half; pat into two greased 9" round cake pans. In a small bowl, beat egg whites until stiff peaks form; spread over dough. Sprinkle with remaining sugar. Bake at 300 degrees for 40 to 45 minutes, or until golden. Cool for 10 minutes before removing from pan to a wire rack. Cool completely. Place one layer on a large serving plate; spread with half the whipped cream. Spoon half the strawberries over cream. Repeat layers. Garnish with mint, if desired. Makes 8 servings.

When time is short, use split biscuits, cubed angel food cake or waffles for a speedy version of strawberry shortcake.

Blueberry Citrus Cake

Rhonda Hauenstein
Tell City, IN

We created this with our love of blueberries and citrus in mind but wanted a light refreshing cake for summer that wasn't too heavy. We entered it in the county fair and received a champion ribbon!

18-1/4 oz. pkg. lemon cake mix
1/2 c. plus 2 T. orange juice
1 c. water
1/3 c. oil
3 eggs, beaten
1-1/2 c. fresh or frozen
   blueberries

1 T. orange zest
1 T. lemon zest
1 c. powdered sugar
Garnish: lemon and orange zest

In a large bowl, combine cake mix, 1/2 cup orange juice, water, oil and eggs. Beat with an electric mixer on low speed for 30 seconds. Increase speed to medium; beat for 2 minutes. With a wooden spoon, gently fold in blueberries and zests. Pour batter into a greased and floured Bundt® pan. Bake for 35 to 40 minutes, or until a toothpick inserted near the center comes out clean. Cool completely in pan on wooden rack. Turn out of pan. Blend remaining orange juice and powdered sugar until smooth; drizzle over cake. Sprinkle with zests. Serves 10 to 12.

Top off desserts with homemade whipped cream...it's really easy to make. Whip one cup heavy cream until soft peaks form, then add one tablespoon sugar and one teaspoon vanilla extract. Continue to whip until stiff peaks form. Delicious!

Berry-Lemon Trifle

Brenda Huey
Geneva, IN

*This was a big hit when I made this for a summer gathering...
there was nothing left to take home!*

14-oz. can sweetened
  condensed milk
8-oz. container lemon yogurt
1/3 c. lemon juice
2 t. lemon zest
8-oz. container frozen whipped
  topping, thawed
1 angel food cake, sliced into
  1-inch cubes

1 c. strawberries, hulled and
  sliced
1 c. blueberries
1 c. peaches, pitted, peeled and
  sliced
Garnish: 1 c. raspberries

Combine condensed milk, yogurt, lemon juice and zest in a large
bowl; fold in whipped topping. In a 3-quart clear glass trifle dish, layer
1/3 each cake cubes, lemon mixture and strawberries. Repeat with
1/3 each cake, lemon mixture and blueberries. Layer remaining cake,
lemon mixture and peaches. Top with additional whipped topping;
sprinkle with raspberries. Cover and refrigerate for at least 4 hours.
Serves 16.

Dress up clear glass trifle dishes, cake plates, even glasses with
water-based acrylic paints...it's easy and clean up is quick! Use paint
brushes or stamps to add designs; let the paint dry thoroughly.
Once dry, set the design by applying a coat of clear acrylic spray
to make the design permanent. Let the sealer dry,
and always wash by hand.

Easy Cherry Ice Cream

Pam Ramsey Elkin
Asheville, NC

Wonderful for a special summer treat. A family favorite that's so easy to make.

2 12-oz. cans evaporated milk
4 c. cherry red pop
2 c. sugar
1 pt. whipping cream

10-oz. jar maraschino cherries,
   drained and chopped
2 to 3 c. milk

Mix together all ingredients except milk. Pour into a 4-quart ice cream maker. Add milk to the fill line. Freeze according to manufacturer's directions as instructed for your ice cream maker. Makes 4 quarts.

Peach Mousse

Faye Mayberry
Saint David, AZ

I am a collector of vintage recipes and love to share the unique recipes that I find. I found this simple recipe in a cookbook compiled by the Infant Welfare Society of Chicago in 1937. A sweet, cool summer treat when peaches are in season.

1-1/2 c. ripe peaches, pitted,
   peeled and mashed
2 c. powdered sugar

1 c. milk
2-1/2 c. whipping cream,
   whipped

Mix together peaches, sugar and milk; fold in whipped cream. Freeze until firm. Serves 10.

Short & sweet...top sliced peaches with a drizzle of honey
and a sprinkling of cinnamon. Yum!

Caitlin's Famous Sour Cream Cake

Wendy Lee Paffenroth
Pine Island, NY

I share this recipe in the memory of Caitlin Hammeran, the daughter of a dear friend. A wonderful young lady, she did it all, and loved cooking. This was one of her favorite recipes.

1 c. butter, softened
1-1/4 c. sugar
2 eggs, beaten
1 c. sour cream
1 t. vanilla extract

2 c. cake flour, sifted
1 t. baking powder
1/2 t. baking soda
Garnish: powdered sugar

Blend together butter and sugar. Add eggs, sour cream and vanilla. Add flour, baking powder and baking soda; mix well. Place half the batter into a greased tube pan. Sprinkle with topping; add remaining batter. Bake at 375 degrees for 40 minutes, or until a toothpick inserted near center comes out clean. Cool in pan for one hour. Invert onto a serving platter; dust with powdered sugar before serving. Serves 10 to 12.

Topping:

1/2 c. chopped pecans or
   walnuts

1/2 t. cinnamon
2 T. sugar

Combine all ingredients in a small bowl.

If you're craving sweet s'mores but it's raining outside, you can still enjoy this ooey-gooey treat. Instead of toasted marshmallows, use marshmallow creme on graham crackers along with a square of chocolate. Microwave on medium-high setting, just long enough to melt the chocolate. Yum!

Debby's Orange Sherbet Cake

Debby Conaway
Cave Spring, GA

This is my most requested cake and also my mom's favorite. I take that as a great compliment because she was an awesome cook. It's so pretty...people are amazed at the beautiful color on the inside.

18-1/4 oz. pkg. orange supreme
  cake mix
6-oz. pkg. orange gelatin mix
12-oz. pkg. frozen sweetened
  flaked coconut
8-oz. container sour cream
16-oz. pkg. powdered sugar

1 t. vanilla extract
2 T. frozen orange juice
  concentrate
12-oz. container frozen whipped
  topping, thawed
Garnish: 3-1/2 oz. can
  sweetened flaked coconut

Prepare cake mix according to package directions; add gelatin mix, blending well. Spread into 3 greased and floured 9" round cake pans. Bake at 350 degrees until golden, 33 to 36 minutes. Cool completely. Mix together remaining ingredients except whipped topping and canned coconut. Mix well; reserve one cup. With a serrated knife, halve each layer horizontally. Spread sour cream mixture between layers, without frosting top. Combine reserved sour cream mixture with whipped topping; mix well. Frost top and sides of cake; sprinkle with remaining coconut. Makes 18 to 20 servings.

A trip to the beach means a collection of seashells and sea glass in all shapes & sizes. Hot glue them to a wooden frame and tuck in a favorite summer vacation photo. Sure to be a sweet memory.

Blackberry Crumble

Marji Nordick
Meridian, ID

My cousins and I used to pick blackberries in Grandma's backyard so she would bake us a crumble. The biggest, juiciest berries were always out of reach, so we had to climb on top of the old shed to get them. They were worth the work, and the scratches from thorns!

1-1/3 c. all-purpose flour	1 qt. blackberries
1/2 t. baking soda	3 T. cornstarch
2/3 c. butter, softened	3/4 c. sugar
1 c. brown sugar, packed	1/8 t. salt
1-1/2 c. quick-cooking oats, uncooked	Garnish: vanilla ice cream or whipped cream

Mix together first 5 ingredients with a fork until pea-sized crumbles form; set aside. Combine remaining ingredients except garnish in a heavy large saucepan. Gently mash some berries, leaving about half of them whole. Bring to a boil over medium-high heat, stirring constantly. Reduce heat to medium; cook until mixture thickens. Pour into a lightly greased 13"x9" glass baking pan; crumble topping over berries. Bake at 350 degrees for 30 minutes, or until lightly golden. Garnish as desired. Serves 8 to 10.

Quick Blackberry Cream Pie

Luda Maurone
Millville, NJ

Using jam makes this a speedy, summertime pie.

1-1/2 c. light cream	3 eggs, beaten
1 t. vanilla extract	9-inch frozen pie crust
12-oz. jar seedless blackberry jam	Garnish: whipped cream, blackberries

Bake crust at 400 degrees for 10 minutes. Whisk remaining ingredients together except garnish; pour into crust. Bake for an additional 10 minutes, until custard jiggles when gently shaken. Cool; garnish as desired. Serves 8.

Very Berry Chocolate Cones

Regina Vining
Warwick, RI

There's a small ice cream shop in a little town not far from our home. They've always carried black raspberry chocolate chunk ice cream... it's my favorite! Last summer, with lots of berries on hand, I created my own version of their berries and chocolate treat...I hope you like it as much as our family does.

8-oz. container sour cream
1/4 c. sugar, divided
zest and juice of 1 lemon,
   divided
1/4 lb. strawberries, hulled and
   quartered, plus 10 whole for
   garnish

1 pt. mixed berries
   (blackberries, blueberries,
   raspberries)
6 1-oz. sqs. milk or dark
   chocolate, coarsely chopped
20 sugar ice cream cones

In a small bowl, combine sour cream, 3 tablespoons sugar, lemon zest and one teaspoon lemon juice. Mix well and refrigerate. In a medium bowl, toss together quartered strawberries and mixed berries with remaining sugar and one to 2 teaspoons lemon juice; refrigerate. Place chocolate in a microwave-safe bowl. Microwave on high, 20 to 30 seconds at a time, until chocolate just starts to melt; stir until smooth. With a pastry brush, paint insides of cones with melted chocolate; place on parchment-lined baking sheet and refrigerate until chocolate hardens, about 15 minutes. To serve, stand cones in narrow glasses. Place a dollop of sour cream mixture in each cone; fill with berry mixture. Top with another dollop of sour cream mixture and garnish with a whole strawberry. Makes 20.

Dip the tops of ice cream cones in melted chocolate, then roll in jimmies, mini chocolate chips or crushed candy. Filled with scoops of ice cream, these cones make any treat extra special!

Bucket-of-Sand Cake

Beth Kramer
Port Saint Lucie, FL

This cake is sure to be a hit at any picnic, cookout or reunion!

8-inch yellow layer cake,
  prepared
24-oz. jar applesauce
1 c. vanilla wafers, finely
  crushed

Garnish: seashell candies,
  gummy fish and sea
  creatures

Cut cake into one-inch cubes. Arrange cubes into a new 8 or 9-cup plastic sandpail, alternating with layers of applesauce. Sprinkle wafer crumbs over top for "sand" and garnish with candies. Serve with a new plastic sand shovel. Serves 10 to 12.

Decorate servings of Bucket-of-Sand Cake with tasty gummy sea creatures. Shop candy stores for colorful seahorses, dolphins and starfish...what fun!

The Summer KITCHEN

Ruthie's Strawberry-Rhubarb Jam

Wendy Jacobs
Idaho Falls, ID

*My neighbor, Ruthie, knows I love strawberry-rhubarb pie, so
she created this recipe when her rhubarb patch was overflowing.
We spent countless sunny afternoons making jam...and memories.*

5 c. rhubarb, chopped
3 c. sugar
3-oz. pkg. strawberry gelatin
   mix

8 1/2-pint canning jars and lids,
   sterilized

In a large saucepan, stir together rhubarb and sugar. Cover; let stand
overnight. Bring rhubarb and sugar to a boil over medium heat.
Reduce heat to low; stirring constantly, simmer for 12 minutes, until
rhubarb is tender. Remove from heat; stir in gelatin mix, mixing well.
Spoon into sterilized jars; secure lids. Refrigerate for up to 3 weeks.
Makes about 8 jars.

The jelly, the jam and the marmalade,
And the cherry and quince preserves she made!
And the sweet-sour pickles of peach and pear,
With cinnamon in 'em, and all things rare!
And the more we ate was the more to spare,
Out to old Aunt Mary's! Ah!

-James Whitcomb Riley

Gooseberry Jam

Mary Beaney
Bourbonnais, IL

A cross between a little something sweet and something tart.

2 qts. gooseberries, hulled and
   chopped
6 c. sugar

1-3/4 oz. pkg. powdered pectin
7 1/2-pint canning jars and lids,
   sterilized

Place berries in a large saucepan over medium heat. Add sugar; mix
well. Bring to a full rolling boil over medium heat; boil one minute,
stirring constantly. Remove from heat; stir in pectin. Skim off foam.
Spoon into hot sterilized jars, leaving 1/4-inch headspace. Wipe
rims; secure with lids and rings. Process in a boiling water bath for
15 minutes; set jars on a towel to cool. Check for seals. Makes 7 jars.

Line a gathering basket with an embroidered tea towel, then tuck
in jars of jams, jellies, biscuits and a favorite cookbook...
a thoughtful gift anyone will enjoy.

County Fair Lime Pickles

Rhonda Hauenstein
Tell City, IN

Growing up, we always looked forward to the county fair. Not only for the rides and the animals, but for the food. Each year we made sure to go to the fish stand for fish sandwiches and their famous lime pickles. I was able to get their recipe a few year ago, and now my daughter and I make these pickles for my parents.

2 gal. cold water
2 c. pickling lime
9 lbs. cucumbers, thinly sliced
ice cubes
3 qts. white vinegar
12 c. sugar

2 T. pickling spice
2 t. canning salt
1 t. mustard seed
1 t. celery seed
10 1-quart canning jars and
    lids, sterilized

Mix together water and lime powder in large 4-gallon crock or 16-quart non-aluminum stockpot. Add cucumbers; cover with ice cubes and let stand, covered, for 24 hours. On the second day, drain cucumbers and rinse thoroughly; wash out crock. Return cucumbers back to clean crock. In a large saucepan, mix remaining ingredients together; cook over medium heat until sugar is dissolved. Pour over cucumbers; cover and let stand for 24 hours. On the third day, transfer cucumbers and syrup to a large non-aluminum pot. Simmer over medium heat for 30 minutes. Spoon cucumbers and syrup into hot sterilized jars, leaving 1/4-inch headspace. Wipe rims; secure with lids and rings. Process in a boiling water bath for 20 minutes; set jars on a towel to cool. Check for seals. Makes 10 jars.

When sharing jars of homemade pickles or preserves, tie on a clever 1st place blue ribbon tag. The tags are easy to find at party supply stores, and make for fun hostess gifts.

The Summer
KITCHEN

Sweet Zucchini Relish

Judy Taylor
Butler, MO

My step-mother got us hooked on this zucchini relish.
My family just won't eat any other kind of relish now.

10 c. zucchini, sliced
3 c. onion, sliced
5 T. canning salt
1 T. cornstarch
2-3/4 c. vinegar, divided
5 c. sugar
1 T. turmeric
1 T. mustard seed or dry
   mustard

Optional: 1 red pepper, finely
   chopped
1 T. celery seed
1/2 t. pepper
1 green pepper, finely chopped
6 1-quart canning jars and lids,
   sterilized

Grind zucchini and onion in a food grinder; add canning salt. Mix well; cover and refrigerate overnight. The next day, drain; rinse twice in cold water. Combine cornstarch with 1/4 cup vinegar in a small bowl; mix well. In large stockpot, mix together sugar, turmeric, mustard seed, red pepper, if using, cornstarch mixture, remaining vinegar, pepper; bring to a boil over medium-high heat. Stir in zucchini mixture and green pepper. Boil for 30 minutes. Spoon into hot sterilized jars, leaving 1/4-inch headspace. Wipe rims; secure with lids and rings. Process in a boiling water bath for 10 minutes. Set jars on a wire rack to cool; check for seals. Makes 6 quarts.

A quick-fix for a bounty of zucchini, this will work great for a favorite zucchini bread recipe. Wash and grate zucchini, then steam for one to 2 minutes. Measure out the amount of grated zucchini a recipe calls for, then spoon into freezer-proof containers, leaving 1/2-inch headspace. Let the zucchini cool, then seal the container and freeze. When ready to use, thaw and discard any liquid.

Roasted Garlic Salsa

Alysson Marshall
Newark, NY

My husband and I love garlic, so we came up with this recipe. It has a nice garlic flavor, but doesn't take away from the salsa.

5 green or orange peppers, chopped
8 banana peppers, chopped
4 jalapeño peppers, chopped
1-1/4 c. garlic, minced
1/2 c. olive oil
19 lbs. roma tomatoes, diced
4 c. onions, chopped
1-1/2 T. chili powder
1-1/2 T. ground cumin
1-1/2 T. dried cilantro
2 t. pepper
2 T. salt
2 T. cayenne pepper
1/2 c. cider vinegar
3 6-oz. cans tomato paste
20 1-pint canning jars and lids, sterilized

Toss together peppers and garlic in oil; spread on large baking sheets. Roast at 350 degrees for 15 minutes. Add all ingredients to a large stockpot. Bring to a boil over medium-high heat; reduce heat and simmer for 15 minutes. Spoon into jars, leaving 1/4-inch headspace. Wipe rims; secure with lids and rings. Process in a boiling water bath for 15 minutes. Set jars on towels to cool; check for seals. Makes 20 jars.

Keep an eye out for vintage silver spoons at flea markets... oh-so clever tied onto giftable jars of salsa, jam, jelly or relish.

The Summer
KITCHEN

Tipton Family Spaghetti Sauce

Doris Tipton
Green Mountain, NC

A friend gave me this recipe many years ago. Now that my daughters are grown, we get together in the summer and prepare this sauce to can..we have a wonderful time together!

1/2 bushel or 30 lbs. tomatoes, peeled and seeded
3 lbs. onions, chopped
1 to 2 c. oil
1/2 c. sugar
1/2 c. canning salt
2 T. dried oregano

2 T. dried basil
Optional: garlic and sweet & hot peppers to taste
4 12-oz. cans tomato paste
10 1-quart canning jars and lids, sterilized

In a large stockpot mix together all ingredients, except tomato paste. Bring to a boil over medium heat. Reduce heat to low; simmer for one hour. Add tomato paste; bring to a boil. Spoon into jars, leaving 1/4-inch headspace. Wipe rims; secure with lids and rings. Process in a boiling water bath for 40 minutes. Set jars on a wire rack to cool; check for seals. Makes 9 to 10 jars.

Give a jar of homemade spaghetti sauce with a glass pantry jar filled with spaghetti, or layer different shapes & sizes of noodles like wagon wheels, rotini, elbow macaroni and shells. What fun!

Raspberry-Jalapeño Jam

Sharon Demers
Dolores, CO

*Because my husband loves raspberries, I created this recipe for him.
If you want to try peaches, my favorite, use one dozen pitted, peeled
and chopped peaches and decrease sugar to 5 to 6 cups.*

5 c. raspberries
7 to 8 jalapeño peppers, chopped
7 c. sugar

1-3/4 oz. pkg. powdered pectin
8 1/2-pint canning jars and lids,
sterilized

Place raspberries in a large saucepan over medium-high heat; cook for
5 to 7 minutes. Mash slightly; add peppers and cook for 15 minutes,
until tender. Add sugar and cook until thickened, about 8 minutes;
add pectin. Cook for an additional 15 minutes, stirring frequently.
Spoon into hot sterilized jars, leaving 1/4-inch headspace. Wipe
rims; secure with lids and rings. Process in a boiling water bath for
20 minutes; set jars on a towel to cool. Check for seals. Makes 8 jars.

Berry Best Freezer Jam

Claire Bertram
Lexington, KY

*When a trip to our local berry farm yielded oodles of fresh berries,
I whipped up this jam so we could enjoy all the fresh flavors together!*

4 c. blueberries, crushed
2 c. raspberries, crushed
5 c. sugar
2 T. lemon juice

3/4 c. water
1-3/4 oz. pkg. powdered pectin
7 1/2-pint freezer-safe plastic
containers and lids, sterilized

Combine blueberries and raspberries in a large bowl. Stir in sugar and
lemon juice. Let stand for 10 minutes. In a small saucepan, bring
water and pectin to a boil. Boil for one minute, stirring constantly.
Add to fruit mixture; stir for 3 minutes. Ladle into freezer containers;
cool to room temperature, about 30 minutes. Cover and let stand
overnight at room temperature before freezing. May be frozen up to
one year. Store in refrigerator up to 3 weeks after opening. Makes
7 containers.

The Summer
KITCHEN

Tart Cherry Salsa

Sharon Jones
Oklahoma City, OK

A really fresh spin on summertime salsas. Remember when cooking with hot peppers to wear rubber gloves to keep the pepper oils off your skin and never rub your eyes.

1-1/3 c. frozen unsweetened
    tart cherries
1/4 c. dried tart cherries,
    coarsely chopped
1/4 c. red onion, finely chopped
1 T. jalapeño pepper, finely
    chopped

1 clove garlic, finely chopped
1 T. fresh cilantro, chopped, or
    1/2 t. dried cilantro
1 t. cornstarch

Let cherries thaw; drain, reserving one tablespoon cherry juice. Chop cherries and combine with onion, jalapeño, garlic and cilantro in a medium saucepan; mix well. Combine reserved cherry juice and cornstarch in a small bowl; mix until smooth. Stir into cherry mixture. Cook, stirring constantly, over medium heat until mixture is thickened; cool. Keep refrigerated. Makes one cup.

Tuck small jars of salsa (and the recipe) inside the pockets of a flowery vintage apron...what a sweet gift!

Aunt Marj's Violet Jelly

Janie Reed
Gooseberry Patch

This sweet memory was shared by Aunt Marj's daughter-in-law, Sally Kinkade. So dear was Aunt Marj to Sally, that she called her Mother. "Mother would go to the woods or fields and pick violets. The jelly she made was so beautiful...a pale liquid lavender you could see right through. She would lovingly pour it into glass jeweled jelly jars. Then there was the label, lettered with her careful calligraphy."

1 qt. fresh violet blossoms,
   stems removed
1 T. lemon juice
1-3/4 oz. pkg. powdered pectin

4 c. sugar
5 1/2-pint canning jars and lids,
   sterilized

Fill a quart jar with violet blossoms. Cover with boiling water; cover tightly and steep for 24 hours. Strain 2 cups of liquid into a large saucepan; discard violets. Add lemon juice and pectin. Bring to a boil over medium-high heat; stir in sugar. Bring to a boil again; boil hard for one minute. Pour into hot sterilized jars, leaving 1/4-inch headspace. Wipe rims; secure lids and rings. Process in a boiling water bath for 15 minutes; set jars on a towel to cool. Check for seals. Makes 5 jars.

As a special delivery for a
friend who loves to garden,
set a jar of jelly inside
a cloth-lined flowerpot.
Tuck in some seed packets
too...she'll love it!

Dandy Dandelion Jelly

Janie Saey
Wentzville, MO

This was my mother's recipe and she was born in 1908. She woke us up many mornings to pick the dandelions for her.

1 qt. fresh dandelion blossoms,
    stems removed
1 qt. boiling water
1-3/4 oz. pkg. powdered pectin

1 t. lemon or orange extract
4-1/2 c. sugar
5 1/2-pint canning jars and lids,
    sterilized

Combine blossoms and water in a large saucepan; bring to a boil over medium heat. Boil for 3 minutes; strain, reserving 3 cups liquid. Discard blossoms. Add pectin, extract and sugar to saucepan; boil for 3 minutes. Pour into hot sterilized jars, leaving 1/4-inch headspace. Wipe rims; secure lids and rings. Process in a boiling water bath for 15 minutes; set jars on a towel to cool. Check for seals. Makes 5 jars.

Set jars of jams or jellies inside a new watering can, then tie on a sunny dandelion bouquet...what a thoughtful housewarming gift!

Pioneer Day Blackberry Jam

Aimee Warner
Gooseberry Patch

When Pioneer Day celebrations begin in July, this scrumptious jam is one we always spread on biscuits we've baked by the campfire.

1-3/4 c. cranberry-raspberry
   juice cocktail
1-3/4 oz. pkg. powdered pectin
3 c. blackberries, crushed

3 c. sugar
4 to 5 1/2-half pint canning jars
  and lids, sterilized

Place juice in a large saucepan; stir in pectin until dissolved. Bring to a full rolling boil over medium-high heat, stirring frequently. Boil hard for one minute, stirring constantly. Remove from heat. Immediately add blackberries; stir vigorously for one minute. Stir in sugar; mix well. Ladle jam into hot sterilized jars, leaving 1/2-inch headspace. Wipe rims, secure lids and rings. Let jam stand in refrigerator until set. May be frozen up to one year. Store in refrigerator up to 3 weeks after opening. Makes 4 to 5 jars.

Tie on an apron and celebrate Pioneer Day, July 24,
with family & friends. Cook over a campfire,
play checkers and enjoy being outdoors.

Homemade Apple Pie Filling

Patti Davis
Kiowa, OK

After I made this recipe using apples that a friend had given me, I have never purchased store apple pie filling again! With this recipe, each fall we can pie filling, then enjoy apple pies and fried apple pies all year long.

4 c. sugar
1-3/4 c. cornstarch
3-1/2 t. cinnamon
1/2 t. nutmeg
3-1/2 t. salt
2-1/2 qts. water

1/4 c. lemon juice
10 lbs. tart apples, cored, peeled
   and sliced into wedges
4 1-quart canning jars and lids,
   sterilized

In a stockpot, mix sugar, cornstarch, spices and salt together. Add water; mix well. Bring to a boil over medium heat; cook until thick and bubbly, stirring frequently. Remove from heat; add lemon juice and set aside. Pack apples into hot, sterilized jars. Pour syrup over apples, leaving 1/2-inch headspace. Draw a non-metallic knife through contents of each jar to remove air bubbles. Wipe rims; secure with lids and rings. Process in a boiling water bath for 10 minutes. Set jars on a towel to cool; check for seals. Makes 4 jars.

Mini pies are especially sweet...share them
on Best Friends Day, June 8.

Teri's Carrot Cake Jam

Teri Johnson
North Ogden, UT

This is a wonderful jam that tastes just like Grandma's carrot cake!

1-1/2 c. carrots, peeled and
  grated
1-1/2 c. pears, cored, peeled and
  chopped
14-oz. can crushed pineapple
3 T. lemon juice
1-1/2 t. cinnamon

1 t. nutmeg
1 t. ground cloves
3-oz. pouch liquid pectin
6-1/2 c. sugar
6 1/2-pint canning jars and lids,
  sterilized

Mix all ingredients except sugar and pectin in a large saucepan. Bring
to a boil over medium heat. Reduce heat to medium-low; simmer for
20 minutes, stirring occasionally. Add pectin and return to a boil. Stir
in sugar; bring to a full rolling boil, stirring constantly. Remove from
heat. Pour into hot sterilized jars, leaving 1/2-inch headspace. Wipe
rims; secure with lids and rings. Process in a boiling water bath for
10 minutes. Set jars on towels to cool; check for seals. Makes 6 jars.

Don't toss plain kraft paper bags...tuck in sheets of cheery
tissue paper, tie on a ribbon and they become
charming gift bags in no time at all!

The Summer
KITCHEN

Spiced Tomato Jam

Carol Anne Barbaro
Clayton, NJ

So delicious...tomatoes make such yummy jam!

3 lbs. tomatoes, peeled, seeded and chopped
1 orange, thinly sliced, seeded and chopped
1 lemon, thinly sliced, seeded and chopped
1 c. sugar
3/4 c. powdered calorie-free sweetener

4-inch cinnamon stick
7 whole cloves
1/2 c. water
1-3/4 oz. pkg. powdered pectin, divided
4 1/2-pint canning jars and lids, sterilized

Combine first 7 ingredients in a large saucepan over medium heat. Simmer for 3 hours, stirring occasionally. In a separate saucepan, mix together water and half the pectin, reserving remaining pectin for another recipe. Bring to a boil over medium-high heat for one minute; add to tomato mixture, mixing well. Spoon into hot sterilized jars, leaving 1/4-inch headspace. Wipe rims; secure with lids and rings. Process in a boiling water bath for 10 minutes; set jars on a towel to cool. Check for seals. Makes 4 jars.

Add a special touch to jars of jams, jellies and salsas...glue a
wooden letter or vintage typewriter key to the jar lid.

Freezer Zucchini Pickles

Barbara Ferree
New Freedom, PA

This recipe comes from my husband's family, where at least two, maybe more, generations have prepared pickles this way. Whenever my in-laws had summer picnics, with anywhere from 60 to 80 people in attendance, these pickles were always enjoyed.

7 c. zucchini, thinly sliced
2 onions, sliced
1 green pepper, chopped
1 t. celery seed
1 t. salt

2 c. sugar
1 c. cider vinegar
7 1-pint freezer-safe plastic
   containers, sterilized

Combine all ingredients except sugar and vinegar in a large bowl. In a separate bowl, mix together sugar and vinegar; stir until sugar dissolves. Add to zucchini mixture; toss to blend. Refrigerate for 24 hours. Spoon into freezer-safe containers. Makes 7 containers.

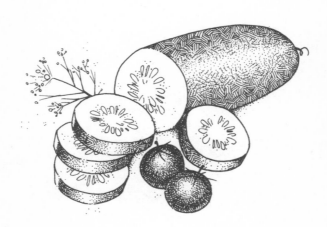

Quick & easy to make, freezer jams and pickles will stay fresh for one year. If you choose to refrigerate them, use within 3 weeks.

Garden Patch Relish

Stacy Jackson
Gooseberry Patch

Growing up, this was one recipe I always looked forward to. Not only because it tasted great, but because we had such fun picking the veggies from our garden. It would be high summer and very hot...we knew at some point Mom would turn on the hose to cool us down, we just didn't know when. I can still hear the squeals and laughter!

4-1/2 c. cucumbers, chopped
3-1/2 c. celery, chopped
3 c. onions, chopped
2 c. red peppers, chopped
1/4 c. canning salt
4 c. water

4 c. cider vinegar
3 c. sugar
2 t. mustard seed
2 t. celery seed
10 1/2-pint canning jars and
   lids, sterilized

Combine cucumbers, celery, onions and peppers in a large bowl; add salt and water. Cover and refrigerate overnight. Drain; rinse and drain again. Combine remaining ingredients in a large kettle; bring to a boil. Add vegetables; simmer for 10 minutes. Ladle hot mixture into hot sterilized jars, leaving 1/4-inch headspace. Wipe rims; secure with lids and rings. Process for 10 minutes in a boiling water bath; set on towels to cool. Check for seals. Makes 10 jars.

Filled with jars of relish, pickles, barbecue sauce, mustard and catsup, a condiment basket is a great gift for anyone who loves summertime grilling. Tuck in a set of tongs, an apron and favorite grilling cookbook...so thoughtful!

Firecracker Hot Pepper Jelly

Lisanne Miller
Canton, MS

About 3 years ago, my father received some pepper plants that were mismarked. To my parents' surprise, what were supposed to be nice sweet banana peppers, turned out to be the very hot and fiery habanero peppers! As one not to waste, my father left a bushel of them at my back door. I decided to put them to good use, and the end result was some of the best hot pepper jelly ever...a true favorite of both my parents!

1 red pepper, cut into wedges
2/3 c. habanero peppers,
   chopped
1-1/2 c. white vinegar

6 c. sugar, divided
2 3-oz. pkgs. liquid pectin
6 to 8 1/2-pint canning jars and
   lids, sterilized

Place peppers and vinegar in a blender; cover and purée. Add 2 cups sugar; blend well. Pour into a large saucepan. Stir in remaining sugar; bring to a boil. Lightly strain mixture, discarding liquid, and return to pan. Stir in pectin. Return to a rolling boil over high heat. Boil for 2 minutes, stirring constantly with a wooden spoon. Remove from heat; skim off foam. Pour into hot sterilized jars, leaving 1/2-inch headspace. Wipe rims; secure with lids and rings. Process for 5 minutes in a boiling water bath. Set jars on a towel to cool; check for seals. Makes 6 to 8 jars.

Savory jams, jellies and butters make tasty appetizers spooned over softened cream cheese and served with crackers. Paired up with a vintage serving spoon tied onto the jar, they're a great hostess gift.

Our Favorite Salsa

June Eier
Forest, OH

Nothing compares to fresh, homemade salsa...you'll never go back to store-bought again!

4 c. tomatoes
2 c. green peppers, chopped
3 29-oz. cans tomato sauce
2 c. onions, chopped
6 to 12 jalapeño peppers,
   chopped
2 T. chili powder
1 T. dried oregano

1 T. ground cumin
1 T. fresh cilantro, chopped
1 T. garlic powder
1 T. red pepper flakes
1 T. salt
1 T. sugar
9 1-pint canning jars and lids,
   sterilized

Bring a large stockpot of water to a boil over high heat. Carefully place tomatoes into stockpot; cook for one minute. Place tomatoes into cold water to cool; peel. Chop and return tomatoes to empty stockpot. Add remaining ingredients; bring to a boil over medium heat. Reduce heat; simmer for 30 minutes. Mix all ingredients together; simmer for 30 minutes. Spoon into hot sterilized jars. Wipe rims; secure with lids and rings. Process for 15 minutes in a boiling water bath. Set on towels to cool; check for seals. Makes 9 jars.

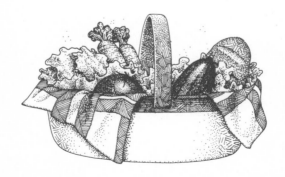

Fill a bushel basket with the flavors of summer...tomatoes, cucumbers, sweet corn, beans, homemade salsa and a Mason jar of lemonade...what a way to welcome new neighbors.

Bread & Butter Pickles

Sharon Welch
Olathe, KS

*Homegrown cucumbers make the best pickles you will ever taste.
My mother shared this recipe with me years ago...she always
had a garden, and at age 90, she still does!*

4 qts. cucumbers, sliced
3 c. onions, sliced
3 cloves garlic, quartered
1/3 c. salt
ice cubes
5 c. sugar

3 c. white vinegar
3 T. mustard seed
1-1/2 t. turmeric
1-1/2 t. celery seed
8 1-pint canning jars and lids,
 sterilized

In a large bowl, mix first 4 ingredients together; cover with ice cubes.
Mix well; let stand for 3 hours. Drain; remove and discard garlic.
Combine remaining ingredients; pour over cucumber mixture. Spoon
into hot sterilized jars, leaving 1/2-inch headspace. Wipe rims; secure
with lids and rings. Process in a boiling water bath for 5 to 8 minutes.
Set jars on towel to cool; check for seals. Makes 8 jars.

Creating a fresh herb wreath is easy...bundle together fresh herbs
like bay leaves, basil, oregano, sage, tarragon & marjoram and
wire onto a straw wreath. Hanging in the kitchen,
it's easy to snip herbs for any recipe.

Picnic Pickles

Lisa Sett
Thousand Oaks, CA

Always a nice gift to share with friends & neighbors.

1/2 c. rice vinegar
1/2 c. sugar
1-quart canning jar and lid, sterilized
2 cucumbers, peeled and thinly sliced
1/2 red, orange or yellow pepper, cut into long strips

1/8 red onion, cut into wedges or strips
Optional: 1 carrot, peeled and thinly sliced
Optional: 1 T. fresh cilantro, chopped

Combine vinegar and sugar in canning jar. Shake, mixing well. Add vegetables to jar in small layers and pack to top. Fill with water to cover vegetables. Replace lid. Turn over jar to mix well. Refrigerate overnight before using. May store in refrigerator for up to one week. Makes one jar.

Don't be shy...enter your best-ever recipe for pickles or salsa in the county fair!

Dixie Tomato Relish

Zoe Bennett
Columbia, SC

There is nothing like the taste of just-picked tomato...juicy and warm from the summer sun. When you make this tomato relish, you can enjoy that fresh flavor year 'round.

2-1/4 lbs. tomatoes
1-1/2 t. lemon zest
1/4 c. lemon juice
6-1/2 c. sugar

1/2 t. butter
2 3-oz. pouches liquid pectin
7 1/2-pint canning jars and lids,
    sterilized

Bring a large stockpot of water to a boil over high heat. Carefully place tomatoes into boiling water; cook for one minute. Place tomatoes into cold water to cool; peel. Chop and return tomatoes to empty stockpot. Bring to a boil over medium heat; reduce heat and simmer for 10 minutes. Measure 3 cups cooked tomatoes and return to stockpot; reserve any remaining tomatoes for a future recipe. Add lemon zest and juice; mix well. Stir in sugar; add butter. Bring mixture to a full rolling boil over high heat, stirring constantly. Stir in pectin. Return to a full rolling boil and boil exactly one minute, stirring constantly. Remove from heat. Skim off any foam with a metal spoon. Ladle into hot sterilized jars, leaving 1/4-inch headspace. Wipe rims; secure with lids and rings. Process in a boiling water bath for 10 minutes. Set on towels to cool; check for seals. Makes 7 jars.

Add a thoughtful jar tie-on to gifts from your kitchen. Use a length of ribbon or rick rack to tie sprigs of rosemary (for remembrance) to jars of jams & jellies before giving.

The Summer
KITCHEN

Green Tomato Jam

Gladys Pilch
Sylva, NC

*When enjoying this jam long after summer's gone, it's sure to be a
reminder of sunny days and trips to the farmers' market.*

8 to 10 green tomatoes
2 lemons, thinly sliced
4 c. sugar
1/4 c. vinegar

1 T. cinnamon
4 1-pint canning jars and lids,
   sterilized

Cover tomatoes with boiling water and let stand 5 minutes; drain.
Thinly slice enough tomatoes to equal 8 cups and place in a stockpot;
add lemon slices. Pour sugar over top. Add vinegar; sprinkle with
cinnamon. Refrigerate mixture overnight. In the morning, cook
rapidly until tomatoes are clear and liquid is like syrup. Pour into hot
sterilized jars and seal. Makes 4 jars.

Invite a few friends over and can or freeze summer's bounty
assembly-line style...everyone will go home with
tasty goodies to fill their pantry.

INDEX

INDEX

INDEX

Send us your favorite recipe!

and the memory that makes it special for you!* If we select your recipe for a brand-new **Gooseberry Patch** cookbook, your name will appear right along with it...and you'll receive a FREE copy of the book.

Share your recipe on our website at
www.gooseberrypatch.com

Or mail to:
Gooseberry Patch • Attn: Cookbook Dept.
2500 Farmers Dr., #110 • Columbus, OH 43235

*Don't forget to include your name, address, phone number and email address so we'll know how to reach you for your FREE book!

Since 1992, we've been publishing country cookbooks for every kitchen and for every meal of the day! Each has hundreds of budget-friendly recipes, using ingredients you already have on hand. Their lay-flat binding makes them easy to use and each is filled with hand-drawn artwork and plenty of personality.

Have a taste for more?

Call us toll-free at
1•800•854•6673

Find us here too!

Join our **Circle of Friends** and discover free recipes & crafts, plus giveaways & more! Visit our website or blog to join and be sure to follow us on Facebook & Twitter too.

www.gooseberrypatch.com

Find us on
Facebook

Follow us on
twitter

Read Our
Blog

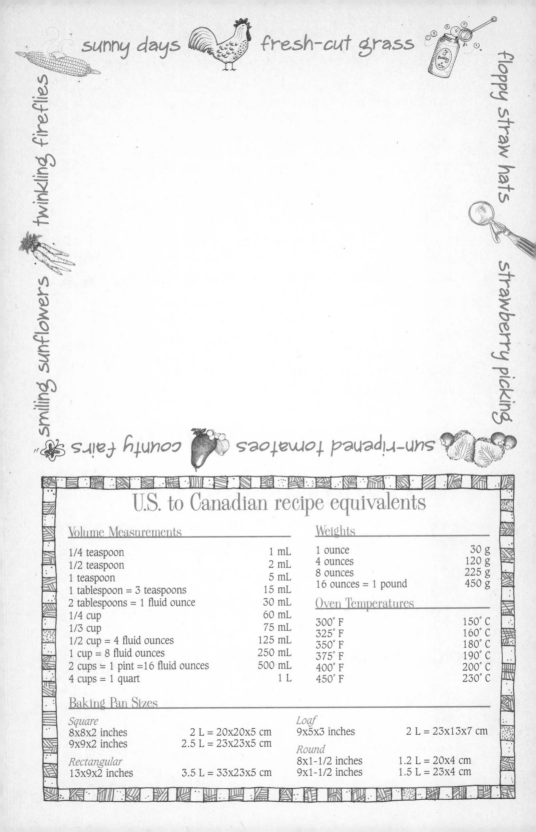

sunny days · fresh-cut grass

floppy straw hats

strawberry picking

twinkling fireflies

smiling sunflowers

"county fairs · sun-ripened tomatoes

U.S. to Canadian recipe equivalents

Volume Measurements

1/4 teaspoon	1 mL
1/2 teaspoon	2 mL
1 teaspoon	5 mL
1 tablespoon = 3 teaspoons	15 mL
2 tablespoons = 1 fluid ounce	30 mL
1/4 cup	60 mL
1/3 cup	75 mL
1/2 cup = 4 fluid ounces	125 mL
1 cup = 8 fluid ounces	250 mL
2 cups = 1 pint =16 fluid ounces	500 mL
4 cups = 1 quart	1 L

Weights

1 ounce	30 g
4 ounces	120 g
8 ounces	225 g
16 ounces = 1 pound	450 g

Oven Temperatures

300° F	150° C
325° F	160° C
350° F	180° C
375° F	190° C
400° F	200° C
450° F	230° C

Baking Pan Sizes

Square
8x8x2 inches	2 L = 20x20x5 cm
9x9x2 inches	2.5 L = 23x23x5 cm

Rectangular
13x9x2 inches	3.5 L = 33x23x5 cm

Loaf
9x5x3 inches	2 L = 23x13x7 cm

Round
8x1-1/2 inches	1.2 L = 20x4 cm
9x1-1/2 inches	1.5 L = 23x4 cm